Praise for *Devotions for Dads*

"Rick Wertz is a man of passion. He has 'been there, done that and has the t-shirt'. His passion to serve the Lord and to reach men for Christ to be better men and fathers is reflected in his writings. This book is written man-to-man and is filled with godly truths saturated with years of experience. You will love it!"
Buddy Griffin, Men's Minister, Sagemont Church, Houston, Texas
National Coalition of Men's Ministry 'Men's Pastor of the Year – 2007'

"In my home I have used these excellent devotions first for my personal devotion time and then to supplement brief daily devotion time with my teenage son. Our faith is nurtured by reflecting on the examination of the meaning of fundamental words - powerful words like discipline, commitment, relationship, covetous, faith, anger, accountable and guidance."
Charlie Smith – dad

"Over the years I have benefited from meeting weekly one-on-one with my best friend and accountability partner. We have gone through a number of men's Bible studies and books targeting men/family issues. The *Devotions for Dads* have also been used in our discussions and often point us back in the right direction, on track with walking the walk as men, husbands and fathers. These devotions are truly a blessing and a useful tool for us guys as they help make the impact of our discussions more profound."
Bill Mohr – dad

"Having been Rick's pastor, I have watched with awe and admiration as he has responded faithfully and courageously to the calling of his ministry with dads. Being with Rick, he exudes the humility of one who has been there for the struggle and the passion of one that lives daily out of his love for God. Both are equally evident in these devotions. I am certain every dad who reads *Devotions for Dads* will be both challenged and encouraged."
Morris Matthis, Senior Pastor
Christ United Methodist Church, Sugar Land, Texas

Devotions for Dads

'...dads becoming heroes.'

Rick Wertz

E-BookTime, LLC
Montgomery, Alabama

Devotions for Dads

Library of Congress Control Number: 2009901823

ISBN: 978-1-60862-010-4

First Edition
Published March 2009
E-BookTime, LLC
6598 Pumpkin Road
Montgomery, AL 36108
www.e-booktime.com

To my family, Linda, Amanda and Tom for their love and support throughout this project. And to Mary Carroll Wertz, my mother, for her prayerful support over the years.

Contents

Introduction

Devotions for Dads was developed over several years as a tool for personal reflection and family devotion by Rick Wertz with the Faithful Fathering Initiative in Texas as part of FFIT's ongoing work with dads. The original inspiration for this book was research published by the Center for Alcohol and Substance Abuse showing that "eating dinner together as a family" is the single most effective way to keep kids off drugs. Statistics show that children who have dinner with their family just once a week are twice as likely to use drugs as children that have dinner with their family five times a week. FFIT asked: How much more could a weekly 30-minute family discussion impact the kids, especially one referencing the word of God and its practical application today? As he began to formulate the Devotions, Rick introduced their use into FFIT's workshops, studies and retreats, and the reception from the dads was very strong. He routinely receives calls and emails from men sharing how they use the Devotions beyond the original goal to enhance their:

- Personal devotion time;

- Devotion and discussion with their wives on topics never broached before; and

- Men's small group meetings and studies.

Each devotion offers five dimensions through which to view a given word or topic. The first is a time of reflection on years past; second is a perspective in the present times; third is a personal point of view with an opportunity to rank your dad or father-figure and compare that ranking to your own today; fourth is a perspective from the timeless word of God; and fifth is time in prayer for specific guidance on your journey as a father. At the end of each week's devotion, there is a sentence for you to finish - 'This week I am encouraged to:'

Our prayer at the Faithful Fathering Initiative in Texas is that the Lord will encourage you through the weekly devotions that make up *Devotions for Dads* and equip you well through the resultant discussions to grow as a faithful father, a dad that prioritizes physical presence, is engaged emotionally and leads spiritually by example.

1. FATHER – Heavenly Father's representative in the home.

As you prepare for this devotion time, prayerfully reflect on a time during your childhood when your dad lowered the boom on you. What was the situation? Did you hit your brother or sister? Did you talk back to your mom? Or did you just push the wrong buttons at the right time? What were the consequences of your actions? What was your perspective on your dad's actions at the time? What is your perspective as an adult reflecting back on the role your dad played in the home?

Father:

Times like these: Looking back at the past generation, dads kept the job description simple – financial provider and disciplinarian of last resort. Looking at television today, dads are portrayed as disengaged at best and bumbling idiots at worst. Looking at the family today, kids need dads that are committed to their mom in marriage and engaged in their lives physically, emotionally and spiritually. What about in your life – Are you intentional about growing in your role as a father? What about in your family – Are you present physically, engaged emotionally and leading spiritually? Do you prioritize the role of a father over your other roles today? Discuss.

Father per Webster's New World Dictionary – *a man who has engendered a child; a man as he is related to his child; a stepfather; a person regarded as a male parent; protector.* What does 'father' bring to mind for you? Is he simply the man that *engendered a child?* Was your dad a good *protector?* What does 'father' mean to your wife?

Rate the following for your dad or father-figure on a scale of 1-10: with 1 being 'low' and 10 being 'high' on his effort as a father to:
- Encourage you in interests and activities;   ___ ___
- Affirm you in growth and accomplishments as you matured;   ___ ___
- Convey his commitment to your mom in marriage;   ___ ___
- Build on his relationship with his father; and,   ___ ___
- Reflect his relationship with Jesus the Christ in the home,
  church and community.   ___ ___

Rate the above again for you today. How do the numbers compare?

The Word on *father* is:

Scripture – John 20:17 *Jesus said, 'Do not hold on to me, for I have not yet returned to the Father. Go instead to my brothers and tell them, 'I am returning to my Father and your Father, to my God and your God.'*
- Share a personal story of how your dad, or someone close to you exemplified the role of a father.

Reflecting on scripture:
- Why did Jesus say, *'Do not hold on to me'*?
- What is significant about the statement that He had *'not yet returned to the Father.'*?
- Who are *'my brothers'*?
- What was conveyed when Jesus said, *'I am returning to my Father and your Father,'*?
- While many men have been blessed with an earthly father that set a great example, many have not. Most fall somewhere between. But all dads have the Heavenly Father to lean on to fill any gap that exists through the brotherhood Jesus the Christ granted us upon His resurrection.

Prayer: Lord, thank You for the many gifts and blessings in my life. I praise You for my wife and mother of our children, and for the children You have blessed me with. Guide me in my efforts to be the husband and father my family needs. Strengthen my relationship with You, that it will be a growing relationship reflected in my marriage daily. Help me be intentional in my efforts to be present physically, engaged emotionally and lead spiritually as Your representative in my family. Amen.

This week I am encouraged to:

_____

_____

_____

_____

_____

_____

_____

2. FAMILY – An ark in the storm.

As you prepare for this devotion time, prayerfully reflect on your family and/or extended family. Did your family have an influence on you? on your friends? in the neighborhood? Identify specifics – Did friends enjoy time in your home; or did you prefer going to your friends' homes? Did you enjoy a peace and comfort in your family; or did you seek that with friends or extended family? What provided the peace and comfort for you?

Family

Times like these: In a generation past, shows like 'Father Knows Best' and 'Leave It to Beaver' were popular and reflected solid American families. Do you remember them? How about the more recent 'Bill Cosby Show'? Each of these shows consistently reflected two things in every episode: a rock-solid marriage relationship and the family eating dinner together. When the 'Bill Cosby Show' was cancelled, one reason given was that the show no longer reflected the family of today. So today, we have 'The Simpsons'. Enough said. What is the word on family today? Is a strong marriage foundational for relationships in the family? Does family time, or lack thereof have an influence on other relationships in our lives? Discuss.

Family per Webster's New World Dictionary – *all the people living in the same house; a social unit consisting of parents and the children they rear.* What does 'family' bring to mind for you? Is there a *social* responsibility for mom and dad to *rear* their children? To *rear* is to build, to grow, to bring to maturity by educating and nourishing – How did your family *rear* you? Share some of your experiences growing up.

Rate the following for your dad or father-figure's legacy of family that you are building upon on a scale of 1-10, with one being a 'weak legacy' and 10 being a 'strong legacy':
- A solid marriage relationship with your mom; ___ ___
- A home of encouragement and support; ___ ___
- A good balance of appropriate affection and effective discipline; ___ ___
- A self-discipline grounded in a growing relationship with Jesus the Christ; and, ___ ___
- A church home as an extension of your family. ___ ___

Rate the above again for your home today. How do the numbers compare?

The Word on *family* is:

Scripture – Gen. 6:14-18 *'Make for yourself an ark of cypress wood; you shall make the ark with rooms, and shall cover it inside and out with pitch. ... the length of the ark three hundred cubits, its breadth fifty cubits, and its height thirty cubits. ... I will establish My covenant with you; and you shall enter the ark – you and your sons and your wife, and your sons' wives with you.*

- Share a personal story of someone who reflected a high level of commitment to building his family, grounded in faith, and how that impressed you. Share the impact that had on you.

Family analogies with the ark in scripture:

- Make an ark 300X50X30 cubits – Marriage and family that will stay strong through the storm;
- Pitch on the outside – Discipline in Christ to keep worldly influences in check;
- Pitch on the inside – Integrity of family, grounded in faith, reinforcing discipline;
- With rooms – Provision for the next generation;
- We are called to build up a family that will have a Christian influence in the world.

Prayer: Lord, thank You for the blessing that is family. Help me understand and step up to the physical, social and spiritual responsibilities as the husband and father You call me to be. I know that in Your strength I can build a family that will stand firm against the storms of life, a legacy to continue for generations. Forgive me my trespasses, and help me forgive those that trespass against me. Lead me not into temptation, but deliver me from evil, that my family may be an ark on top of the flood waters of worldly influence, by Your grace and for Your glory. Amen.

This week I am encouraged to:

_____

_____

_____

_____

_____

3. DISCIPLINE – Got some?

As you prepare for this devotion time, seek clarity on the impact that discipline, or the lack thereof, had on your formative years and beyond. Reflect on a couple of specific situations: one where a valuable life lesson was learned; and, another where the discipline did not necessarily fit the crime. I remember a buddy and I being asked by a store clerk if we were going to pay for the candy bars in our pockets. Parents were called and a life lesson was certainly learned. Did you ever 'get away' with something, only to learn a very painful lesson later?

Discipline

Times like these: Society seems completely undisciplined. In the headlines, we see a man in the highest office of the land lie under oath; We see respected corporate leaders misrepresenting the company's performance; We see pastors that lead churches having adulterous affairs; We see the commitment between man and woman in marriage barely holding on 50% of the time; We see men failing to step up to the responsibility of fatherhood 40% of the time; And we see behavioral problems in our schools occurring at record levels. What about in your life – What is your reference for discipline? What about in your family – Do you have rules established in the home, and consequences for breaking those rules? Discuss.

Discipline per Webster's New World Dictionary – *training that develops self-control, character*. What does 'discipline' bring to mind for you? Did you receive some 'hands on' *training* from Dad? Did spankings play a role in helping you *develop self-control?* How was your *character* shaped by the enforcement of rules in the home? Share some of your experiences growing up.

Rate the following for disciplinary guidelines in your home growing up on a scale of 1-10, with one being 'no discipline' and 10 being 'rigid discipline' in the area of:
- Showing respect to each member of your family; ___ ___
- Doing your chores/accepting responsibilities around the home; ___ ___
- Having good study habits/getting homework done; ___ ___
- Being home ahead of any curfew set; and, ___ ___
- Honoring your mother and father. ___ ___

Rate the above again for your home today. How do the numbers compare?

The Word on discipline is:
Scripture – John 15:1-2 *'I am the true vine, and my Father is the gardener. He cuts off every branch in me that bears no fruit, while every branch that does bear fruit he prunes so that it will be even more fruitful.'*
- Share a personal story of being disciplined by your dad or father figure. What impact did it have on you?

Reflecting on the scripture:
- If God is the *gardener* and Jesus is the *vine*, who are the branches? Fruit?
- Why is it necessary to cut some branches off and prune others?
- How does this relate to discipline in the home? How about self-discipline?
- How does this relate to our lives as Christians?
- The journey is to Christ-likeness. There is much cutting and pruning to be done along the way to facilitate walking closer to Him tomorrow than today.

Prayer: Lord, thank you for the timelessness of Your Word. It does define and encourage discipline in an undisciplined world. Grant me the wisdom to discern the right things to do and the discipline to do them. Help me lead my family by example day by day in a disciplined lifestyle that glorifies You. When I fall, grant me the humility to ask forgiveness. Amen.

This week I am encouraged to:

_____

_____

_____

_____

_____

_____

_____

_____

4. AFFECTION – Honoring God.

As you prepare for this devotion time, reflect on the way your parents showed their affection for each other and for you. Did they hug each other? Did they kiss in front of you? Were hugs in your home spontaneous? Did you marry a hugger? Reflect also on what television conveyed to you as a kid in the way of open affection. What has influenced your definition of appropriate affection today?

Affection:

Times like these: In the headlines, we see two men hugging in celebration of their 'wedding' in San Francisco. On national television, prime time, we see two female pop artists open mouth kissing. On regular television we see movies with bedroom scenes. At the theater, there is a lot of skin and explicit sex scenes in 'PG13' rated movies. And in the halls of schools, we see kids intimately embraced and kissing at every opportunity before school, between classes and after school. What about in your life – What is the word on affection today? What about in your family - What is your reference for appropriate affection in the home and outside the home?

Affection per Webster's New World Dictionary – *fond or tender feeling; warm liking.* What does 'affection' bring to mind for you? Is it a comforting hug? What *fond or tender feelings* have you experienced recently? How did you express those feelings? Is it appropriate to put a hug on someone you have a *warm liking* for? Share some of your experiences growing up.

Rate the following for the home in which you grew up on a scale of 1-10, with one being never and 10 being all the time:
- Mom and Dad openly hugged and kissed;   ___ ___
- Mom gave hugs to the kids;   ___ ___
- Dad gave hugs to the kids;   ___ ___
- Family did not watch movies in the home that had
  bedroom scenes; and,   ___ ___
- You were not allowed to go to movies that had explicit
  sex scenes.   ___ ___

Rate the above again for your home today. How do the numbers compare?

The Word on affection is:
Scripture – 1 Corinthians 6:19-20 *'Do you not know that your body is a temple of the Holy Spirit, who is in you, whom you have received from God? You are not your own; you were bought at a price. Therefore honor God with your body.'*
   - Share your thoughts on open affection between adults that would 'honor God'.

Affection is intended to be the physical, emotional and spiritual affirmation that:
   - You honor the *temple of the Holy Spirit;*
   - You love your wife as Christ loves the church;
   - Your son is a strong and healthy young man, who controls his feelings, and with whom you are well pleased;
   - Your daughter is a beautiful young woman inside and out, who is worth fighting for, and with whom you are well pleased;
   - You cherish the blessing of family.

Prayer: Lord, thank you for the timelessness of Your Word. As the world shows increasing tolerance to inappropriate affection, I know I am responsible for my family and for showing the appropriate affection that will ground my children in Your love. Enable me to become the affectionate and loving husband and father you have called me to be. Amen.

This week I am encouraged to:

_____

_____

_____

_____

_____

_____

_____

_____

5. LISTENING – Say what?

As you prepare for this devotion time, reflect on the way your voice was respected as a child growing up. Did your parents give you an opportunity to voice your opinion? Did they show appreciation for your point of view? Were you given the chance to explain your side of the story? Reflect also on your schooling as a kid. Did the teacher welcome questions and dialogue, or was it a 'speak when spoken to' classroom? What are the qualities of someone you respect as a good listener?

Listening:

Times like these: With technology came the microchip and the nanosecond. The microchip holds more memory than a room full of computers did just 15 years ago, and the nanosecond has been referenced as the attention span of the next generation. And we of the present generation have come to form opinions and make decisions based on 15-second news bites. Over the last 10 – 15 years various media have bombarded our homes with an overwhelming volume of information 24/7 working to inform a society that as a whole does not listen well. How about in your life - Do you consider yourself a good listener? How about in your family – Do you listen well at home? Do you put down the paper and turn off the television at dinnertime? Discuss.

Listen per Webster's New World Dictionary – *to make a conscious effort to hear; attend closely.* What does 'listen' bring to mind for you? Was your dad a good listener? Did he *make a conscious effort to hear* your input when it came to rules, curfews and consequences in the home? Did you *attend closely* during father/son talks about relationships? Or were conversations one-sided?

Rate the following for the home in which you grew up on a scale of 1-10, with one being 'never' and 10 being 'all the time':
  - Family ate dinner together at least five times a week;   ___ ___
  - Children could express their points of view freely;   ___ ___
  - Dad was approachable for one-on-one discussions;   ___ ___
  - Dad encouraged discussion about performance in
    school and other activities; and,   ___ ___
  - Dad led a family devotion and prayer time every week.   ___ ___
Rate the above again for your home today. How do the numbers compare?

The Word on listening is:

Scripture – James 1:19-20 *'My dear brothers, take note of this: Everyone should be quick to listen, slow to speak and slow to become angry, for man's anger does not bring about the righteous life that God desires.'*
- Share an experience when the failure to listen well led to a heated exchange, possibly even anger. What impact did that have on you?

Listening is intended to be the dimension of communication that conveys:
- a respect for the one speaking;
- a sincere effort to understand another point of view;
- the patience to hear fully what is going to be said;
- an interest in another's perspective and opinion; and
- the love of Jesus the Christ.

Prayer: Lord, You know I can be quick to speak and even quicker to become angry. Forgive me. Help me be quick to listen and slower to speak in my discussions with my children and with their mother. Guide me in becoming more open and approachable anytime about anything. Amen.

This week I am encouraged to:

_____

_____

_____

_____

_____

_____

_____

_____

_____

_____

_____

6. INVOLVEMENT – Who knows your voice?

As you prepare for this devotion time, prayerfully reflect on how you use your time – work, commute, hobbies, sports activities, television, time with family, time with kids one-on-one. Identify specifically what takes up significant blocks of time on weekdays and weekends. Does the amount of time spent in the respective areas represent the priorities you want to pass on to your children? What are your priorities today?

Involvement:
Times like these: Commute time has men leaving before the children wake up and returning after they've gone to bed. Job requirements often include a good bit of travel. Companies mandate 24/7 availability complete with accessibility via pager and cell phone. Long hours and shift work keep dads out of sync with kids' activities. What about your life – Do you have one? What about your family – What is the word on involvement in your home today? Is it limited to weekend activities?

Involvement per Webster's New World Dictionary – *to enfold or envelop; to include by necessity; to relate to or affect.* What does 'involvement' bring to mind for you? Did your parents *relate to or affect* your interests and activities? Did they help you find and nurture your unique gifts? Share some of your experiences growing up.

Rate the following for your dad when you were growing up on a scale of 1-10, with one being 'no involvement' and 10 being 'very involved' by:
- Supporting interests and activities;   ___ ___
- Knowing your teachers and coaches;   ___ ___
- Helping with homework;   ___ ___
- Teaching you a skill and/or a sport; and   ___ ___
- Sharing life lessons.   ___ ___

Rate the above again for your home today. How do the numbers compare?

The Word on involvement is:
Scripture – John 10:2-5 *'The man who enters by the gate is the shepherd of his sheep. The watchman opens the gate for him, and the sheep listen to his voice. He calls his own sheep by name and leads them out. When he has brought out all his own, he goes on ahead of them, and his sheep follow him because they know his voice. But they will never follow a stranger; in fact, they will run away from him because they do not recognize a stranger's voice.'*
- Share a personal story of a day you and your dad or father figure spent together, and the impact it had on you.

Reflecting on the scripture:
- What is significant about *the man who enters by the gate?*
- In a fathering context, who are the sheep? Who is leading?
- Why do the sheep *know his voice?* Who is the *stranger*?
- How does this relate to the level of involvement in your home?
- As the Lord's representative in the home, the dad is the shepherd of his children, and they need to know his voice. Otherwise, the stranger will distract them.

Prayer: Lord, thank you for the timelessness of Your Word. I know my children will only know my voice if I am present and accounted for in their lives day by day. Guide me in my effort to balance life's priorities in favor of the family You have blessed me with. Help me become the husband and father you have called me to be. Amen.

This week I am encouraged to:

_____

_____

_____

_____

_____

_____

_____

_____

7. COMMITMENT – To priorities.

As you prepare for this devotion time, prayerfully reflect on how you were influenced by someone's commitment to you, the family, their work or their faith. Identify specifics around what impressed you about their commitment. Did the commitment reflect their priorities in life? Do those close to you know what you are committed to?

Commitment:

Times like these: Approximately half of all marriages fail. The popular trend of living together without marriage fails at an even higher rate. Some activists are working to redefine marriage to be more inclusive of homosexual and polygamous relationships, but these historically reflect even a lower level of commitment. What about your life – does commitment have an impact on your relationships today? What about your family - does commitment to the marriage relationship have an impact on the family? Discuss.

Commitment per Webster's New World Dictionary – *a pledge or a promise to do something.* What does 'commitment' bring to mind for you? What *pledge or promise* have you made lately? Did you follow through and *do something?* What lessons do you recall learning from your parents in the area of commitment? Share some of your experiences growing up.

Rate the following for your dad when you were growing up on a scale of 1-10, with one being 'no commitment' and 10 being 'absolute commitment' to:
- Education; minimum of a high school diploma;   ___ ___
- Completing a tough season with the team;   ___ ___
- Attending church regularly;   ___ ___
- The marriage relationship with your mother; and,   ___ ___
- Growing in his walk as a Christian man, husband
  and father.   ___ ___

Rate the above again for your home today. How do the numbers compare?

The Word on commitment is:

Scripture – Gen. 2:24 *'For this reason a man will leave his father and mother and be united to his wife, and they will become one flesh.'* Mal.2:15 *'Has not the Lord made them one? In flesh and spirit they are his. And why one? Because he was seeking godly offspring. So guard yourself in your spirit, and do not break faith with the wife of your youth.'*

- Share a personal story of someone close to you that exemplifies a strong commitment to the marriage relationship, and the impact that had on you.

Reflecting on the scripture:

- What is significant about leaving your *father and mother?*
- Does *be united*, and *become one flesh* reflect a level of commitment to a relationship?
- What is the purpose of this relationship?
- What impact does the marriage relationship have on the next generation?
- Commitment is foundational in relationship – with Jesus the Christ, in marriage and in family.

Prayer: Lord, I know commitment to my relationship in marriage is the reflection of my relationship with You to my children. Forgive me where I have fallen short. May my commitment to You be contagious through my commitment in marriage, that the home You have blessed me with will provide fertile soil for 'godly offspring'. Help me become the husband and father you have called me to be. Amen.

This week I am encouraged to:

_____

_____

_____

_____

_____

_____

_____

8. CONSISTENCY – Knowing what to expect.

As you prepare for this devotion time, prayerfully reflect on how you were influenced by someone's consistent character and presence in your immediate or extended family. Identify specifics around what impressed you about their consistency in the family, workplace or church. Did their consistency provide a reliable point of reference for you? Do those close to you see you as a reliable point of reference today?

Consistency:

Times like these: A job or career change looms on the horizon. Busyness and travel with work dictates a dad's presence, or lack thereof, in the home. The kids' schedules are demanding. Multiple activities take mom and dad in different directions. Having dinner together as a family just isn't doable. Going to church together as a family is doable, if there isn't a soccer or baseball tournament. What about in your life - What is the word on consistency amid the hectic pace you keep today? What about in your family – Would your kids describe you as consistent in your schedule, moods and priorities? Discuss.

Consistency per Webster's New World Dictionary – *holding always to the same principles or practice.* What does 'consistency' bring to mind for you? What are you *holding always to?* What *principles or practice* guide you in setting priorities? What lessons do you recall learning from your parents in the area of consistency? Share some of your experiences growing up.

Rate the following for your dad or father-figure during your formative years on a scale of 1-10, with one being 'inconsistent' and 10 being 'very consistent' in:
- His job/career and work schedule;   _____
- His hobbies and interests;   _____
- His moods and character;   _____
- His respect for your mother; and,   _____
- His walk with Christ.   _____

Rate the above again for your home today. How do the numbers compare?

The Word on consistency is:
Scripture – Exodus 33:14 *'The Lord replied, 'My Presence will go with you and I will give you rest.'*
- Share a personal story of someone that was consistently present in your life, someone you wanted to follow. What impact did they have on you?

Reflecting on the scripture:
- Why is the Lord's *Presence* so important to Moses?
- Do you think Moses felt affirmed as God's man?
- What kind of *rest* is God speaking of?
- What is significant about the Lord's reply to Moses?
- The Lord's consistent presence with Moses gave him peace of mind amidst the trials and tribulations of leading a stiff-necked people.

Prayer: Lord, thank You for Your truth, a constant point of reference in a challenging world. Reflecting Your truth through consistency in my schedule, character, moods, ethics and faith gives my family a solid reference point and a peace of mind in these confusing times. As I rest in You, I will become a more consistent physical, emotional and spiritual presence in the home you have blessed me with. Amen.

This week I am encouraged to:

_____

_____

_____

_____

_____

_____

_____

_____

_____

9. AWARENESS – Who do you know?

As you prepare for this devotion time, prayerfully reflect on how you felt when you were caught doing something you shouldn't have been doing. Identify specifics – what you were doing, why you were doing it, and why you were caught? Did 'getting caught' provide a valuable lesson in life for you? How did your dad, mom and/or family handle the situation?

Awareness:
Times like these: Mom and Dad both have demanding jobs outside of the home. When they have the time, they don't have the energy to be engaged with their kids late in the evening. Kids are often leaving an empty house when they go to school, and returning to an empty house after school. The void that used to be family time is filled with television, the internet, computer games and friends. What about in your life – Are you aware of what priorities are driving your life? What about in your family – Are you aware of your children's world; and, do they know you? Does awareness, or lack thereof have an influence on relationships in the family? Discuss.

Awareness per Webster's New World Dictionary – *on one's guard; vigilant; knowing or realizing; conscious; informed.* What does 'awareness' bring to mind for you? What are you *on one's guard* about? What do you make a *conscious* effort to be *informed* on? What lessons do you recall learning from your parents in the area of awareness? Share some of your experiences growing up.

Rate the following for your dad or father-figure during your formative years on a scale of 1-10, with one being 'unaware' and 10 being 'very aware' of:
- Your world at school, who your friends were;   ___ ___
- Your feelings about teachers, coaches;   ___ ___
- Your hobbies and interests;   ___ ___
- Your strengths and weaknesses; and,   ___ ___
- Your walk with Christ.   ___ ___
Rate the above again for your home today. How do the numbers compare?

The Word on awareness is:

Scripture – John 10:14-15 Jesus says, *'I am the good shepherd; I know my sheep and my sheep know me – just as the Father knows me and I know the father...'*

- Share a story about someone who was aware of a situation you were in as a kid and provided valuable guidance that kept you away from trouble. Share the impact they had on you.

Reflecting on the scripture:

- Who is *the good shepherd?*
- How does he *know* his sheep?
- How do the sheep *know* him?
- What is the analogy to the father/child relationship?
- We are to know our children as the Father knows His Son, and our children are to know us as Jesus knows His Father.

Prayer: Lord, I praise You and thank You for Your word and Your love. You have blessed me with people in my life that have known me and have provided guidance in times of trial. I ask that You equip me to be more aware of my children's world. Help me be more available and accessible for them in any time of need. I want to be a father that knows his family, and whose family knows him. Forgive me for the fronts I put up, the masks I put on. Enable me to be real, that my family will always be well aware of who I am and Whose I am. Amen.

This week I am encouraged to:

_____

_____

_____

_____

_____

_____

_____

_____

10. PERSEVERANCE – Cal who?

As you prepare for this devotion time, prayerfully reflect on a time when you 'stuck it out' through a tough Little League baseball season; a tough class in high school or college; or a tough time in a close relationship. Identify specifics – how close were you to throwing in the towel; what told you to press on? With the benefit of hindsight, what is your perspective on that situation today? How did your dad, mom and/or family influence the situation?

Perseverance:
Times like these: Cal Ripken Jr.'s 2632 consecutive baseball games played serves as a model for perseverance and is seen as an unbreakable record by today's athletes. He effectively worked over 16 years without missing a day for the company he started with out of school! In contrast, most of us will change companies five times during the course of a career. What about in your life – Do you give in to the aches and pains associated with the daily routine and 'throw in the towel'? Or do you press on through troubles on the job, or in a relationship? What about in your family – How do you exemplify perseverance at home? What is your reference for perseverance in life?

Perseverance per Webster's New World Dictionary – *to continue in some effort, course of action, in spite of difficulty, opposition; steadfast in purpose; persist.* What does 'perseverance' bring to mind for you? Have you recently *continued in some effort in spite of difficulty*? What have you been *steadfast in purpose* about? Did your parents stress the need to *persist* when the going got tough? Share some of your experiences growing up.

Rate the following for your dad or father-figure's influence during your formative years on a scale of 1-10, with one being 'threw in the towel' and 10 being 'persevered through':
- A sports season with a coach that 'wasn't fair';   ___ ___
- A tough teacher/class in high school or college;   ___ ___
- A disagreement with the pastor or in the church;   ___ ___
- A challenging time on the job or with a boss; and   ___ ___
- A death in the family that raised questions about God.   ___ ___
Rate the above again for your home today. How do the numbers compare?

The Word on *perseverance* is:

Scripture – Rom. 5:3-5 '*...but we also rejoice in our sufferings, because we know that suffering produces perseverance; perseverance, character; and character, hope. And hope does not disappoint us because God has poured out his love into our hearts by the Holy Spirit, ...*'
- Share a personal story of someone who persevered through a tough situation when you were a kid and how that impressed you.

Reflecting on the scripture:
- What does it mean to *rejoice in our sufferings?*
- Why is *sufferings* plural??
- What kind of *character* is He building? Is it applicable in these times?
- Has *hope* ever disappointed you?
- We are called to persevere with the eternal perspective always in focus.

Prayer: My Father, Who art in heaven, hallowed be Your name. I praise You for the physical, emotional and spiritual trials You have blessed me with. Thank you for strengthening me through my sufferings, teaching me to persevere, and building the character You call me to reflect. Grant me power through the Holy Spirit to run the good race with the hope of spending eternity with You. Help me become the man, husband and father that reflects that hope at every turn. Amen.

This week I am encouraged to:

_____

_____

_____

_____

_____

_____

_____

11. RELATIONSHIP – Be real!

As you prepare for this devotion time, prayerfully reflect on your relationship in marriage and/or the relationship between your mother and father. Did your folks' relationship have an influence on you? Identify specifics – Was there trust in the relationship; did they show respect for each other; was there a mutual commitment to the relationship? Are trust, respect and commitment foundational to your idea of, or expectations in a relationship?

Relationship:

Times like these: Less than half of all households in the USA are occupied by married couples – a record low. Relationships in 50%+ of families are severed by divorce. Young men and women are waiting longer to marry, and many see 'living together' as an acceptable altern-ative to marriage. Relationships among peers are sometimes superficial. Even relationships with friends often stay on the surface, or are guarded. Are real relationships possible today? What is a 'real' relationship? Discuss.

Relationship per Webster's New World Dictionary – *connection or association, as by origin or kind; connection by kinship or marriage; or the same family.* What does 'relationship' bring to mind for you? Is there a hunger for *connection* in the home, in the church and at work? A *real* relationship has a maturity that can provide emotional balance in the ups and downs of life – Did you see this at work in your family? Share some of your experiences growing up.

Rate the following for your dad or father-figure's relationships on a scale of 1-10, with one being a 'weak relationship' and 10 being a 'strong relationship':
- With friends, other men;   ___ ___
- With extended family;   ___ ___
- Within the family, yourself, brothers and/or sisters;   ___ ___
- In marriage with your mom; and,   ___ ___
- With Jesus the Christ.   ___ ___

Rate the above again for you today. How do the numbers compare?

The Word on *relationship* is:

Scripture – 1Peter 3:7 *'...live with your wives in an understanding way, ...and show her honor as a fellow heir of the grace of life, so that your prayers will not be hindered.*

- Share a personal story of how your dad, or someone close to you honored his wife, and how that impressed you. Share the impact that had on you and your understanding of relationship.

Reflecting on scripture:

- What does *in an understanding way* mean to you?
- Are you seeking to know your wife better tomorrow than today?
- Does your marriage relationship reflect *the grace of life* God has planned for you?
- Is the relationship with your wife an extension of your relationship with Jesus the Christ?
- Do you think family is designed to impact the next generation's understanding of relationship?

Prayer: Lord, my kids get a lesson in relationships every day. It is in the home that children get their first exposure to relationships between adults; between a man and a woman; between a husband and a wife; and, between a dad and a mom. And it is in the home that they gain perspective on a healthy relationship between an adult and a child. The day to day experiences in the home are foundational for the next generation's perspective on relationship. Lord, help me embrace that responsibility. May the relationships in the home You have blessed me with reflect my growing relationship with You. Guide me in living with my wife 'in an understanding way', that we may pass on the 'grace of life' to the next generation by Your grace and for Your glory. Amen.

This week I am encouraged to:

_____

_____

_____

_____

_____

_____

12. CONTENTMENT – Being under the influence.

As you prepare for this devotion time, prayerfully reflect on your needs and/or the needs of your family while growing up. Did your folks' meet your daily needs? Identify specifics – What were your needs from their perspective; what were your needs from your perspective; was there clarity between needs and wants? What perspective do you reference when you discern between needs and wants in your life today?

Contentment:

Times like these: The minimum down payment on a home mortgage has moved steadily from 40% to 20% to 10% to 0% across the last 30 years. New cars can be purchased with no money down and no interest for one to five years. Furniture stores advertise 0-0-0 for no money down, no interest and no payment until next year! Debt appears to no longer be an obstacle between needs and wants. What about in your life - Is there any difference between needs and wants today? What about in your family – Do you discuss contentment in your home? Discuss.

Contentment per Webster's New World Dictionary – *having or showing no desire for something more or different; satisfied.* What does 'contentment' bring to mind for you? Is there a hunger for *something more* in your life, in your home, or at your place of work? Is being *satisfied* today seen as complacency? Did you see *contentment* at work in your family while growing up? Share some of your experiences.

Rate the following for your dad or father-figure's level of contentment in his life on a scale of 1-10, with one being a 'desire for something more' and 10 being 'satisfied':
- With the ability to provide for his family;   ___ ___
- With the size of the family home;   ___ ___
- With the number of cars, and types of cars in the driveway;   ___ ___
- With his relationship in marriage; and,   ___ ___
- With his understanding of God's will for him.   ___ ___

Rate the above again for you today. How do the numbers compare?

The Word on *contentment* is:
Scripture – Ephesians 5:17-18 *'Therefore do not be foolish, but understand what the Lord's will is. Do not get drunk on wine, which leads to debauchery. Instead, be filled with the Spirit.'*
- Share a personal story of how your dad, or someone close to you understood where the Lord had him and why. Share the impact that had on your understanding of contentment versus complacency.

Reflecting on scripture:
- What *foolish* paths has world led you down?
- Does it seem pretty easy *to get drunk* on wants?
- Are you able to define the line between contentment and complacency?
- Are you under the influence of the Holy Spirit in discerning the Lord's will for you?
- Trust that needs will be met in relationship with Jesus the Christ by the power of the Holy Spirit.

Prayer: Lord, You know what I want, and You know what I need. You know the temptations I face. Help me discern clearly day by day between what the world announces as needs and what Your word has to say about my needs. Guide me in my need for a growing relationship with You, that I may gain understanding of Your will for me. Keep me under the influence of the Holy Spirit, that through me You will protect my family from being under the influence of wants in the world. Lord, help me stand firm, grounded in Your word, content in who I am, Whose I am and what I have in You. Amen.

This week I am encouraged to:

_____

_____

_____

_____

_____

_____

_____

13. TRUTH – Absolute versus relative.

As you prepare for this devotion time, prayerfully reflect on a tough situation you were in when you told the truth and/or didn't tell the truth while growing up. Did your folks' stress truthfulness in the home? Were there repercussions when you got caught not telling the truth? Identify specifics – Was there a standard set for telling the truth in the home; what discipline was enforced as a result of the standard set; what was the 'truth' standard'? Do you carry a 'truth' standard forward in your life today?

Truth:

Times like these: 'It depends what your definition of is, is.', the infamous line spoken by President Clinton under oath, provided a glimpse of the 'state of truth' today. Whether in a court of law, on a tax return, or in a simple discussion, it appears that the truth depends on someone's interpretation, or is simply relative to a given situation. What about in your life - Is there such a thing as absolute truth today? What about in your family – What is the reference for determining/ascertaining truth in your home? Discuss.

Truth per Webster's New World Dictionary – *statement, etc. that accords with fact or reality; an established or verified fact, principle.* What does 'truth' bring to mind for you? When you pick up the paper, or turn on the television, do you trust the media will convey *established or verified fact?* Is there a desire for well-grounded *principle* in your life, in your home, or at your place of work? Is being *truthful* today seen as naive? Did you see the *truth* as foundational with communication in your family while growing up? Share some of your experiences.

Rate the following for your dad or father-figure's level of truthfulness in his life on a scale of 1-10, with one being 'not truthful' and 10 being 'absolutely truthful':
  - With stories from his youth;   ___ ___
  - In daily communication with friends and family;   ___ ___
  - In honoring the demands of his work schedule;   ___ ___
  - With declarations when filing his annual tax return; and,   ___ ___
  - With his consistent reference to absolute truth in the
    word of God, scripture.   ___ ___
Rate the above again for you today. How do the numbers compare?

The Word on *truth* is:

Scripture – John 14:6 *'Jesus answered, 'I am the way and the truth and the life. No one comes to the Father except through me."*

- Share a personal story of how your dad, or someone close to you stood firm in absolute truth. What impact did that have on your understanding of being grounded in scripture.

Reflecting on scripture:
- How many *ways* does Jesus refer to?
- How many *truths* are there?
- What *life* is Jesus speaking of?
- Is scripture, the word of God, indeed meant to be the absolute truth for all time?
- As you walk with Jesus, seeking truth in the Father, you will find life in the Holy Spirit.

Prayer: Lord, You know I live in a relative world with few absolutes. Thank You for Your son Jesus the Christ, for Your word and for the Holy Spirit. You have provided the Trinity as the absolute in this relative world. Guide me in my walk with Jesus; equip me in Your word, which is Truth; and strengthen me in the Holy Spirit to stand firm in You. Lord, help me reflect Your absolute truth at every turn and be a positive influence in this world for the sake of my family and the generations to follow. Amen.

This week I am encouraged to:

14. ENGAGEMENT – Physical, emotional and spiritual.

As you prepare for this devotion time, prayerfully reflect on a situation when, as a kid, you put up a pretty good front only to be busted by your mom or dad. Were you convinced that they had eyes in the back of their heads or spies in the neighborhood? Did your folks have that insight straight through to your heart? Identify specifics – What were you trying to cover – a bad report card; a fight you were in; or, a poor choice that caused some trouble? Was it your eyes or your mannerisms that gave you away? Or did they just know you and know something was up?

Engagement:
Times like these: Kids today are involved in all kinds of activities beyond school, from soccer to piano and from baseball to band. And parents are physically engaged in getting the kids more involved. It seems this generation is destined to pass on busy-ness as its legacy. In the process parents may know what their kids can do, but do they *know* their kids? Are physical activities and schedules dominating relationship development in the family? Is there a balance of emotional engagement with relationships in the home? Is there a healthy dimension of spiritual engagement?

Engage per Webster's New World Dictionary – *to pledge oneself; promise; involve oneself; undertake; take part; be active; to interlock; mesh.* What does 'engage' bring to mind for you? Is it primarily a physical dimension of engagement, *taking part, being active* in your child's life? Or is it a good balance of physical, emotional and spiritual engagement? What is your perspective on the engagement level of your parents during your formative years? Share some of your experiences.

Rate the following for how engaged your dad or father-figure was in your life on a scale of 1-10, with one being 'not engaged' and 10 being 'over engaged' in:
- Helping you learn to ride a bike;   ___ ___
- Your school work, academic development;   ___ ___
- Your athletic interests and activities;   ___ ___
- Your physical and emotional maturity; and,   ___ ___
- Your spiritual maturity.   ___ ___

Rate the above again for you today. How do the numbers compare?

The Word on *engagement* is:

Scripture – Deut.6:6-9 *'These commandments that I give you today are to be upon your hearts. Impress them on your children. Talk about them when you sit at home and when you walk along the road, when you lie down and when you get up. Tie them as symbols on your hands and bind them on your foreheads. Write them on the doorframes of your houses and on your gates.'*

- Share a personal story of how your dad, or someone close to you who was, or was not, engaged in your spiritual growth. Share the impact that had on your relationship with Jesus the Christ.

Reflecting on scripture:
- How are you to *impress them on your children?*
- Will your family listen to what you say, or catch what you've got?
- Is God referring to your activities on Sunday?
- Will spiritual engagement with your family impact the generations to follow?
- A generation is in the balance and dads being engaged tip the balance toward Him.

Prayer: Lord, You know the busy-ness I live with in the world. Help me discern the right priorities in my life, that I may balance physical, emotional and spiritual engagement in the home You have blessed me with. I want to know my kids, and I want my kids to know me. Lord, strengthen my marriage and relationships in the home for the sake of raising of a godly generation by Your grace and for Your glory. Amen.

This week I am encouraged to:

_____

_____

_____

_____

_____

_____

_____

15. ENCOURAGEMENT – Beyond the trophies.

As you prepare for this devotion time, prayerfully reflect on a situation when you made an error on the ball field. What was your dad's response? How about when you made the principal's honor roll? Do you remember a time when you brought a bad test grade or report card home? What was conversation like at the dinner table? Was there encouragement, or criticism? How has the way your parents encouraged you influenced the way you encourage others today?

Encouragement:
Times like these: Trophy sales are at all-time highs with every kid on the team getting a trophy. Self-esteem seems to be the key concern of many parents and schools today. Individual awards and recognition are sometimes minimized, if not eliminated, for the sake of everyone's self-esteem. What is the purpose in giving trophies for participation in an activity? Is this the way kids are encouraged and prepared for challenges ahead on the road of life? Encouragement is a way to guide children through ups and downs, recognize successes and failures, and put emphasis on the journey of nurturing unique giftedness. What about in your family – Is encouragement tempered with healthy review and critique? Discuss.

Encourage per Webster's New World Dictionary – *to give courage, hope, or confidence to; embolden; hearten; to give support to; be favorable to.* What does 'encourage' bring to mind for you? How did dad and mom *give courage, hope* to you and your siblings in the home? Is it common in your place of work for employees *to give support, be favorable to* each other? Do you find it easier to encourage, or to be critical of someone? Share some of your experiences.

Rate the following for your dad or father-figure's level of encouragement through your formative years on a scale of 1-10, with one being 'over critical' and 10 being 'very encouraging' of your:
- Academic performance;   ___ ___
- Athletic development;   ___ ___
- Accepting of responsibility;   ___ ___
- Choice of friends; and,   ___ ___
- Spiritual growth and maturity.   ___ ___

Rate the above again for you today. How do the numbers compare?

The Word on *encouragement* is:

Scripture – Phil.4:6 *'Do not be anxious about anything, but in everything, by prayer and petition, with thanksgiving, present your requests to God. And the peace of God, which transcends all understanding, will guard your hearts and your minds in Christ Jesus.'*
- Share a personal story of how your dad, or someone close to you kept a failure in perspective. Share the impact that had on you and your understanding of encouragement.

Reflecting on scripture:
- What are you *anxious about?*
- How is your *prayer* life?
- Why are we to present requests *with thanksgiving?*
- What is significant about the instruction *by prayer and petition?*
- As you let go, turn it over to Him by *prayer and petition*, the *peace of God* will be present.

Prayer: Lord, You know that I tend to be anxious about failure, particularly when it comes to my kids. Instead of seeking greater control over my child's experiences with success and failure, help me seek understanding of how You are working through those experiences. Equip me in providing well-grounded encouragement as I guide my family down the road of life. Amen

This week I am encouraged to:

_____

_____

_____

_____

_____

_____

_____

_____

_____

16. COVETOUS – Wants, desires and discipline.

As you prepare for this devotion time, prayerfully reflect on a situation when you didn't get what you wanted for Christmas, but your buddy did. Do you remember being frustrated, even angry that he got something you really wanted? How about today? When you look at your peers, do you compare yourself with what they have, or where they are professionally? Reflect on where that takes you emotionally? Do you consider this healthy competition, or is it something else?

Covetous:

Times like these: The desire for newer, bigger and better stuff is stoked by virtually every marketing effort out there, from the local furniture store dealer to the new home builder to the new car showroom floor. The desire to look younger, slimmer, and more attractive is encouraged by magazine covers, television shows and even doctors' offices. Cosmetic surgery is becoming more common, even for men. The desire to compete at a high level has prompted a number of professional athletes to take performance enhancing drugs. Is this all in the name of betterment, desiring to be the best we can be? What about in your life - When is the line crossed from simply desiring something to coveting that which is not yours to grasp? What about in your family - What is the reference for covetous behavior in the home?

Covet per Webster's New World Dictionary – *to want ardently, especially something another person has; long for with envy; greedy.* What does 'covetous' bring to mind for you? Did an argument with a brother or sister ever start over something you *wanted ardently*? What lessons did dad and mom pass on in the home to you and your siblings when it came to *wanting something another person has*? Are you generally content, or do you have a tendency to *long for* something *with envy*, to covet?

Rate the following for your dad or father-figure's level of covetousness on a scale of 1-10, with one being 'content with his' and 10 being 'covetous of another's':
  - Car;   ___ ___
  - House;   ___ ___
  - Friendships;   ___ ___
  - Marriage; and,   ___ ___
  - Provision for his family.   ___ ___

Rate the above again for you today. How do the numbers compare?

The Word on *covetousness* is:

Scripture – Exodus 20:17 *'You shall not covet your neighbor's house. You shall not covet your neighbor's wife, or his manservant or maidservant, his ox or donkey, or anything that belongs to your neighbor.'*
  - Share a personal story of how your dad, or someone close to you put this 10th commandment to practice. Share the impact that had on you and your understanding of covetousness.

Reflecting on scripture:
  - You are to focus on taking care of your house.
  - Your wife deserves all your love and attention.
  - Do not let things that do not belong to you divert your eyes.
  - Is every want or desire considered covetous behavior?
  - To covet is allowing evil to take a want or desire to a level that distracts us from His purpose.

Prayer: Lord, You know my wants and desires can cross that line to covetousness. Forgive me and help me focus in on the gifts and blessings You have given me, that I may be content with who I am and Whose I am. Protect me from passivity and grant me the boldness and confidence to be all You intend me to become. Help me be the husband and father my family needs. Amen.

This week I am encouraged to:

_____

_____

_____

_____

_____

_____

_____

_____

_____

17. CLEAN HOUSE – Ever take inventory?

As you prepare for this devotion time, prayerfully reflect on a situation during your younger years when you heard your dad use a cuss word; or, when you stumbled across a pornographic magazine. How did you deal with that? Do you remember a time when you were tempted by something you knew was wrong? What influenced your decision to go, or to not go with the temptation? Identify specifics – Did you experience excitement about testing the waters, pushing the envelope? Was there an overriding fear of repercussions? How have your experiences at home and in life equipped you to steer clear of temptations today?

Clean house:

Times like these: Cable and satellite television channels allow virtually anything to flow into homes 24/7. Regular television channels have become more and more suggestive. Even the commercials during regular viewing are often openly salacious. Internet access introduces a whole new medium that can impact the home for good and for bad. Some sports magazines have moved toward soft pornography. And women's apparel magazines show a lot of skin in their marketing efforts. What opened the gate to this barrage of violence, sex, drugs and alcohol that seemingly flows uninhibited into the home? Have you taken inventory lately of what comes into your home and how it gets there? A clean house is a way to set the standard and guide children through the formative years, to recognize and process right from wrong, to recognize and deal with temptations they will face. What is your reference for a clean house? Discuss.

Clean House per Webster's New World Dictionary – *designed to produce and maintain an atmosphere almost 100% free of contaminants; used in the manufacture and assembly of spacecraft, in hospitals, etc.* What does 'clean house' bring to mind for you? How did Dad and Mom *design* the home to minimize the *contaminants* you and your siblings in the home were exposed to? Do you find it easier to design a clean house or a clean office? Share thoughts.

Rate the following for your dad or father-figure's ability to design a clean house through your formative years on a scale of 1-10: with 1 being 'contaminated' and 10 being 'a clean atmosphere':

- Anger; ___ ___
- Foul language; ___ ___
- Alcohol; ___ ___
- Pornographic material; and, ___ ___
- Rocky marriage relationship. ___ ___

Rate the above again for you today. How do the numbers compare?

The Word on a *clean house* is:
Scripture – Deuteronomy 7:26 *'Do not bring a detestable thing into your house or you, like it, will be set apart for destruction. Utterly abhor and detest it, for it is set apart for destruction.'*
- Share a personal story of how your dad, or someone close to you kept, or did not keep alcohol out of the home. Share the impact that had on you.

Reflecting on scripture:
- What is *a detestable thing* today?
- Moses was referring to foreign gods. Are you bringing any foreign gods *into your house?*
- What *will be set apart for destruction?*
- Does a tolerant society encourage us to *utterly abhor and detest* anything?
- As you inventory what enters your house, set a standard that will glorify the Father.

Prayer: Lord, other gods knock on my door constantly. Help me stay clean as a man by turning from the influences of the world by the power of the Holy Spirit. Enable me as a husband and father to establish a clean house, a standard in the home that will glorify You. Amen.

This week I am encouraged to:

_____

_____

_____

_____

_____

_____

_____

_____

_____

_____

_____

18. GIFTS – Identify and nurture.

As you prepare for this devotion time, prayerfully reflect on a time when your father said that you were really good at something. How did that hit you? Do you remember a time when the reverse happened – when you just didn't have the athleticism for football; or, when you didn't have the aptitude for math? How did Dad handle those situations? Reflect on what influenced your decision to go ahead in a sport, or with a particular field of study? Did your home experience equip you in nurturing unique gifts you had been given?

Gifts:

Times like these: Money and expectations of others often are key drivers in decisions our kids make. A daughter studies medicine because her dad wants her to be a doctor. She really wanted to be an elementary school teacher, but he said there wasn't any money in teaching. A son plays football because his dad can't relate to his real passion for theatre. How are doors opened to effective dialogue with kids about their gifts? Athletics are typically a dad's forte. But there must be a balance in the discussions about the academic and spiritual gifts a child possesses as well. As parents our job is to help our children identify their unique gifts, encourage them to accept responsibility for gifts they've been given and guide them in nurturing those gifts to be the best they can be. What is your perspective on how children glorify the Father? Discuss.

Gifted per Webster's New World Dictionary – *having a natural ability or aptitude; talented; notably superior in intelligence.* What does 'gifted' bring to mind for you? How did Dad and Mom help you identify your *natural ability or aptitude?* Did they direct you and encourage you in specific areas where you were seen as *talented?* Share thoughts.

Rate the following for your dad or father-figure's level of focus on identifying and nurturing your unique gifts on a scale of 1-10: with 1 being 'not interested' and 10 being 'high' in the area of:
  - Academics;   ___ ___
  - Athletics;   ___ ___
  - Relationships;   ___ ___
  - Leadership; and,   ___ ___
  - Spirituality.   ___ ___
Rate the above again for you today. How do the numbers compare?

The Word on *gifts* is:

Scripture – Romans 12:5-6 *'so in Christ we who are many form one body, and each member belongs to all the others. We have different gifts, according to the grace given us...'*
- Share a personal story of how your dad, or someone close to you encouraged, or failed to encourage you to develop gifts you were given. Share the impact that had on you.

Reflecting on scripture:
- What *body* is the apostle Paul referring to?
- How do *many form one body?*
- Why is it important that *each member belongs to all the others?*
- What does Paul mean when he says, *We have different gifts, according to the grace given us?*
- Paul goes on to list specific physical, emotional and spiritual gifts some had been given. As we identify, nurture and utilize those unique gifts by His grace, the Father will be glorified.

Prayer: Lord, help me see past the demands of the world. I pray and ask that You grant my children a clear understanding of who they are, Whose they are and how they are to utilize gifts You have given them. And that through their unique gifts they will be a godly influence in the world by Your grace and for Your glory. Amen.

This week I am encouraged to:

_____

_____

_____

_____

_____

_____

_____

_____

_____

19. PRAYER – Got answers?

As you prepare for this devotion time, prayerfully reflect on a time when you prayed fervently for something – a Christmas gift, a position on the team, a relationship. Was your prayer answered? What has influenced your practice of going to the Lord in prayer? Did you grow up in a family that prayed together? Was there a situation in which prayer was the only place to turn? When do you turn to prayer about a situation today? What have you prayed for?

Prayer:

Times like these: As long as there are tests in school there will be prayer in school, but woe to those who pray out loud - a 'moment of silence' is the politically acceptable term. Boys can circle up to pray before a game, but the coach can't lead it - in some school districts the coach can be fired for being present when the kids pray! Meet You at the Pole, and the National Day of Prayer are initiatives to keep prayer at the forefront, yet there are forces actively working to push prayer to the background. How about in your life - Is prayer a part of your day from the start, at the end, at mealtime, before a road trip? How about in your home - Did your mom and dad emphasize prayer in the home, or was it more of a 'church thing'. What is your perspective on when and how to pray on your own, with your wife, with your children, in the church or in the workplace?

Prayer per Webster's New World Dictionary – *an earnest request; supplication; an utterance to God in praise, thanksgiving, confession, etc.; any spiritual communion with God.* What does 'prayer' bring to mind for you? How did Dad and Mom help you pray and discern *an earnest request?* Did they direct you with a balance of *praise, thanksgiving* and *confession* with requests? Was there a formula for prayer or simply *spiritual communion with God?* Share thoughts.

Rate the following for your dad or father-figure's prayer life on a scale of 1-10: with 1 being 'never' and 10 being 'very often' that you saw him:
- In prayer;   ___ ___
- Lead the family in prayer;   ___ ___
- Lift up prayer concerns in and outside the family;   ___ ___
- Practice the discipline of prayer and scripture daily; and,   ___ ___
- Volunteer as a prayer partner with someone or as a member of a prayer team.   ___ ___

Rate the above again for you today. How do the numbers compare?

The Word on *prayer* is:
Scripture – Mark 11:24, Jesus said, *'Therefore I tell you, whatever you ask for in prayer, believe that you have received it, and it will be yours.'*
- Share a personal story of how your dad, or someone close to you prayed fervently for something but didn't get the answer desired. Share the impact that had on you.

Reflecting on scripture:
- What is significant about Peter being the one to receive this word from Jesus?
- What is the difference between something you ask for and something *you ask for in prayer?*
- What is it that we are to *believe?*
- When *you have received it,* is *it* always what you expected? Any thoughts on why or why not?
- *It will be yours* is Jesus' promise to Peter and it is a promise to us. In prayer we enter communion with God by the power of the Holy Spirit and gain greater understanding of His will.

Prayer: Lord, help me pray as You taught Your disciples to pray. My father Who art in Heaven, hallowed be thy name. Thy kingdom come, Thy will be done on earth as it is in Heaven. Give us this day our daily bread and forgive us our trespasses, as we forgive those who trespass against us. And lead us not into temptation, but deliver us from evil. For Thine is the kingdom and the power and the glory forever. Amen.

This week I am encouraged to:

20. FAITH – In something.

As you prepare for this devotion time, prayerfully reflect on a situation when you turned to your faith and trust in God – a broken relationship, a health concern, a tragedy. Was there a peace in your heart? Reflect also on what you put your faith in as an adult – do you have faith in job security; financial security? When are you able to let go and let God? What has influenced the practice of your faith? Identify specifics – Did you grow up in a family that attended church? Has your faith in God ever seen you through a difficult time?

Faith:

Times like these: We are a diverse people living in a very litigious society. Faith expressed in the workplace can result in 'disciplinary action up to and including termination'. Yet it appears mandatory for us to have faith in our employer for a paycheck, our doctor for good health, our government for a secure city and nation! Expressing secular faith doesn't seem to be a problem, but expressing Christian faith can be. We all have faith in something, and expression of that faith influences those around us. What about in your life - Is your faith in Jesus the Christ evident? What about in your home - Did your mom and dad have a faith that was contagious? What is your perspective on how your faith is to be reflected in the home, in the church and in the workplace?

Faith per Webster's New World Dictionary – *unquestioning belief that does not require proof or evidence; anything believed; complete trust, confidence, or reliance; allegiance to; loyalty....* What does 'faith' bring to mind for you? How did Dad and Mom reflect their faith? Was it an *unquestioning belief?* Did they encourage *complete trust, confidence, reliance* in faith? Was there a forum in your home that allowed a dialogue about faith? Share thoughts.

Rate the following for your dad or father-figure's willingness/tendency to share his faith in Jesus the Christ on a scale of 1-10: with 1 being 'never' and 10 being 'always' when he was:
  - In the home;   ___ ___
  - At church;   ___ ___
  - With extended family;   ___ ___
  - In the workplace; and,   ___ ___
  - In the neighborhood and/or community.   ___ ___
Rate the above again for you today. How do the numbers compare?

The Word on *faith* is:

Scripture – Romans 15:13, *'May the God of Hope fill you with all joy and peace, in believing, that you may abound in hope by the power of the Holy Spirit.'*

- Share a personal story of how your dad, or someone close to you called on their faith in a time of trial. Share the impact that had on you.

Reflecting on scripture:

- Why does Paul make reference to God as the *God of Hope*?
- Have you ever been filled *with all joy and peace*?
- How are *joy and peace* realized *in believing*?
- What is the relationship between *in believing* and *by the power of the Holy Spirit*?
- *The God of Hope* is our Heavenly Father; *in believing* is reference to Jesus the Christ; and *the power of the Holy Spirit* completes the triune God. It is through the Trinity, that we realize *all joy and peace*, and abound in *hope*.

Prayer: Lord, most days I have faith in You. But sometimes I'm the man I have faith in. The distractions are many and the choices are not always obvious. Grant me the strength and discernment to choose You whenever a choice needs to be made. Help me grow in my faith that I may let go and let You be God in my life, my family, my church. Amen.

This week I am encouraged to:

_____

_____

_____

_____

_____

_____

_____

_____

_____

_____

21. FUN – Have some!

As you prepare for this devotion time, prayerfully reflect on a time during your childhood when you had fun with your family – a nightly wrestling match with Dad, a trip to a ball game, a special vacation. Was something special going on in your heart? Reflect also on what fun is to you as an adult – do you have fun with your wife, in the home, at work? What do you do for fun? What has influenced your ability to have fun? Identify specifics – Did you grow up in a family that had fun together? Or was it all work and no play? Did you think Christians were allowed to have fun?

Fun:

Times like these: "My son turned 10 just the other day. He said, 'Thanks for the ball Dad, come on let's play. Can you teach me to throw?' I said, 'Not today. I've got a lot to do.' He said, 'That's okay.' He walked away but his smile never dimmed. He said, 'I'm gonna be like him.'" – from Harry Chapin's 1974 hit song, 'Cat's in the Cradle'. There is a reason that song has weighed so heavily on my heart over the years. It seems sometimes a man can get so caught up in this performance-driven culture and all the 'important stuff' he does that the most important things get overlooked – like enjoying family, having fun with his kids. What about in your home – Did you have some fun times in your family? Did your mom and dad dedicate time for trips to the park or beach just to have fun together as a family? What do you do for fun today?

Fun per Webster's New World Dictionary – *lively play or playfulness; amusement, sport, recreation, etc.; enjoyment or pleasure; a source or cause of amusement or merriment.* What does 'fun' bring to mind for you? Did you have fun competing in a *sport*? What kind of *recreation* did Dad and Mom encourage? Was it okay to have *lively play* in the home? Was there an element of *enjoyment or pleasure* in the church as you learned about faith? Share thoughts.

Rate the following for your dad or father-figure's tendency to be able to enjoy the moment, even laugh out loud, on a scale of 1-10: with 1 being 'low' and 10 being 'high' when he was:
- At the dinner table; ___ ___
- On a family outing or trip; ___ ___
- Playing or watching competitive sports; ___ ___
- In the workplace; and, ___ ___
- In the church, in Sunday school or participating in a work project. ___ ___

Rate the above again for you today. How do the numbers compare?

The Word on *fun* is:

Scripture – John 10:10 Jesus' words, *'The thief comes only to steal and kill and destroy; I have come that they may have life, and have it to the full.'*
- Share a personal story of how your dad, or someone close to you enjoyed their life *to the full*. Share the impact that had on you.

Reflecting on scripture:
- Who is the *thief*?
- What does he come *to steal and kill and destroy*?
- What does Jesus mean when He says, *'I have come that they may have life,'*?
- What is having life *to the full*? Have you ever thought of Jesus having fun, smiling?
- Life is fun when I am under the influence of the Holy Spirit. It's when I am under the influence of something else that I let the thief twist and distort my perspective on life.

Prayer: Lord, thank You for the freedom You offer – freedom to choose, freedom to love, freedom to laugh, freedom from my sins. Help me embrace fully the freedom You offer, and enjoy the relationship You call me to. That, under the influence of the Holy Spirit, I may be a fun-loving and contagious Christian in my family, my church, my community as I enjoy life to the full by Your grace and for Your glory. Amen.

This week I am encouraged to:

22. ANGER – Do not let the sun go down!

As you prepare for this devotion time, prayerfully reflect on a time at home when you saw frustration percolate to anger in your family – an argument between Dad and an older sibling, a door slammed, a voice raised. Do you remember a quiet that followed? Reflect also on when you have crossed the line to anger as an adult – do you have 'hot buttons' that your wife and/or kids have a knack for pushing? What do you find frustrating? What has influenced your ability to control your anger? Did your dad have a temper or get angry often?

Anger:
Times like these: A dad, angry at calls made during a Little League Baseball game, punches an umpire with his fist. A batter, after being hit by a pitch, charges the mound in anger and hits the pitcher. Dad, after a rough day at the office, yells at his teenage son to straighten up his room. His son yells back at him and in a split second they're toe to toe. In a rage just short of hitting the boy, Dad says, 'Get out of my house and stay out!' And his son did. What is it that causes a normal person to cross the line to anger? What about in your home – Did you see your parents argue? Do you, or your wife, have a temper that flares up on occasion? How are disagreements handled in your family? What is your perspective on anger as a Christian? Discuss.

Anger per Webster's New World Dictionary – *a feeling of displeasure resulting from an injury, mistreatment, opposition, etc., and usually showing itself in a desire to fight back at the supposed cause of this feeling.* What does 'anger' bring to mind for you? Did you have any *feelings of displeasure* as a child in your home? How did Dad and Mom encourage you to *fight back* against *this feeling?* Was the *supposed cause* always in the proper perspective, or had frustration distorted reality? Does frustration always percolate into anger? Share thoughts.

Rate the following for your dad or father-figure's ability to keep his anger in check on a scale of 1-10: with 1 being 'not at all' and 10 being 'completely in check' when he was:
- Participating in a competitive activity;   ___ ___
- A spectator at one of your competitive activities;   ___ ___
- Arguing with you, or another sibling;   ___ ___
- Frustrated with his day at work; and,   ___ ___
- Disagreeing with your mom over a family issue.   ___ ___

Rate the above again for you today. How do the numbers compare?

The Word on *anger* is:

Scripture – Eph.4:26-27, *'In your anger do not sin. Do not let the sun go down while you are still angry, and do not give the devil a foothold.'*
- Share a personal story of how your dad, or someone close to you lost, or maintained control in his anger. Share the impact that had on you.

Reflecting on scripture:
- Is *anger* a sin?
- What does Paul mean by *in your anger do not sin?*
- Why is it important to *not let the sun go down while you are still angry?*
- How can we *give the devil a foothold?*
- Only Jesus can be angry at the right person, at the right time, to the right degree, for the right reasons, and have the right impact. The rest of us are to lean on Him before we reach the point of anger.

Prayer: Lord, thank You for being You. You know my tendency to cross the line from frustration to anger quickly. Help me be more sensitive to the frustration that pushes me to that line. When I do cross the line, and doors slam physically, emotionally or spiritually, grant me the strength to knock and open them before the sun goes down. Amen.

This week I am encouraged to:

_____

_____

_____

_____

_____

_____

_____

_____

_____

_____

23. REAL – To be or not to be.

As you prepare for this devotion time, prayerfully reflect on a time during your school years when you were told to just be yourself – encouraging words from Mom, advice from Dad, concern from a teacher or coach about the group you were hanging with. Do you remember how you responded? Who knows you well enough today to offer sincere encouragement or advice? What has influenced your ability to just be yourself, to be real as a man today? Identify specifics.

Real:

Times like these: A celebrity news anchor dies and the knowledge of a secret life with a second wife and family surfaces - Did anyone know the real man? A pastor falls from grace - Did the church ever know the real man. Dad feels pressure to be one man at home, a different man at church, and yet a different man at work - Some days he wonders if he knows the real man! What is it that causes men to put up fronts powerful enough to cause such confusion? How about in your life – Do pressures at work and at home take you outside yourself? Do you have Christian brothers who know you well and hold you accountable on a weekly basis? What about your family - Do your wife and children see the same man at home that you are at church and at work? What is your reference for, or perspective on being real as a Christian man? Discuss.

Real per Webster's New World Dictionary – *actual; true, objectively so; authentic; genuine; not merely seeming, pretended, imagined.* What does 'real' bring to mind for you? Can you recall what was *actual* and *true* as a child in your home? How did Dad and Mom encourage you to not *pretend* to be someone you weren't? Did peer pressure, or possibly early success, tempt you to act differently than your *authentic, genuine* self? Share thoughts.

Rate the following for your dad or father-figure's ability to be real on a scale of 1-10: with 1 being 'low' and 10 being 'high' when he was:
- With friends and family;   _____
- At work;   _____
- At home;   _____
- Discussing life with you during your teenage years; and,   _____
- At church and/or in Sunday school.   _____

Rate the above again for you today. How do the numbers compare?

The Word on *real* is:

Scripture – John 8:44, Jesus to the Pharisees *'You belong to your father, the devil, and you want to carry out your father's desire. He was a murderer from the beginning, not holding to the truth, for there is no truth in him. When he lies, he speaks his native language, for he is a liar and the father of lies.'*

- Share a personal story of how your dad, or someone close to you stood firm under pressure for what was right and true, grounded in who he was and Whose he was. Share the impact that had on you.

Reflecting on scripture:

- Were the Pharisees being real with each other and with God or religious to a fault?
- How can the religious elite come to *belong to the devil?* Does it happen today?
- How can righteous men get distracted by the one *not holding to the truth?*
- How clever it was of the devil to operate under the guise of the Pharisees. How did that happen?
- You can fool some of the people all the time, and all of the people some of the time. But Jesus knows the real you. He calls us to be real in our walk with Him at home, at church and at work.

Prayer: Lord, thank You for being You. Guide me in a growing relationship with You, that I may be well-grounded in who I am and Whose I am. Help me be the same man at home, at work and at church. Surround me with Christian brothers that will hold me accountable to be real, to stay on the narrow path when the confusion of the world tries to lead me elsewhere. Amen.

This week I am encouraged to:

_____

_____

_____

_____

_____

_____

_____

24. FAITHFUL – With a few things.

As you prepare for this devotion time, prayerfully reflect on a time when your dad or mom faithfully woke you up for school every day. Do you recall how your parents performed a variety of duties and provided for your needs just as a part of their routine? What motivated them to do that? And reflect on your parents' marriage relationship. Is faithful one of the words that comes to mind to describe the relationship they exemplified? What has influenced your perspective on being faithful as a man today? Identify specifics.

Faithful:
Times like these: The day to day pressures in our success-driven culture can be overwhelming. It helps me to look at life from the perspective of the farmer – He works the ground, plants the seed, irrigates and even sprays for pests. Is he guaranteed success of a high-yield crop? No. But if he doesn't work the ground, fails to plant the seed, doesn't irrigate, and decides not to spray for pests, what is he guaranteed? Failure. Success can be a by-product of being faithful in the role you are in, but it isn't a given, and it shouldn't be the driver. How about in your life – Do pressures to succeed have hold of you? What is the difference between being 'driven to be successful' and 'driven to be faithful'? Is your focus at home on being successful or being faithful in your marriage and family relationships? What is your reference for, or perspective on being faithful as a Christian man?

Faithful per Webster's New World Dictionary – *maintaining allegiance to someone or something; constant; loyal; having or showing a strong sense of duty or responsibility; conscientious.* What does 'faithful' bring to mind for you? Can you recall *maintaining allegiance* to your parents? Did your dad have a *strong sense of duty* to your family? Did your mom and dad provide a *constant* point of reference with their marriage relationship? Share thoughts or experiences.

Rate the following for your dad or father-figure's level of focus on being faithful on a scale of 1-10: with 1 being 'low' and 10 being 'high' as a:
- Friend; ___ ___
- Co-worker; ___ ___
- Husband; ___ ___
- Father; and, ___ ___
- Christian man. ___ ___

Rate the above again for you today. How do the numbers compare?

The Word on *faithful* is:

Scripture – Matt.25:23, *'Well done, good and faithful servant. You have been faithful with a few things; I will put you in charge of many things. Come and share in your master's happiness.'*

- Share a personal story of how your dad, or someone close to you stayed faithful to a company, to a ministry or to his family through tough times. Share the impact that had on you.

Reflecting on scripture:

- What makes a servant *good and faithful?*
- Was the servant put *in charge of many things* because of his success or his faithfulness?
- Is the *master* a results-oriented boss?
- Is *come and share your master's happiness* the kind of recognition typically expected?
- A good and faithful servant focuses on the task at hand, with God's reward in mind.

Prayer: Lord, thank You for being faithful. Mother Theresa once said, 'We are not called to be successful. We are called to be faithful', suggesting that we are to leave the rest to You. Lord, equip me to be more like the farmer, to be faithful where You have me, to walk the walk You have me on, and to know that You are God and I am not. Amen.

This week I am encouraged to:

_____

_____

_____

_____

_____

_____

_____

_____

_____

25. CHOICE – Making the right one.

As you prepare for this devotion time, prayerfully reflect on a time as a boy when you made a bad choice, and your dad introduced you to the consequences of your choice. Reflect also on your high school years, your prom night and/or graduation night – when you faced tough situations, did you make good decisions? Do you recall some examples set in the home by your parents? Did you have family discussions about choices and consequences? What has influenced your perspective on making good choices as a man today? Identify specifics.

Choice:

Times like these: Whatever looks good, feels good and is available NOW can influence the choices we make across the day. Terms requiring 'no money down' for even the most major purchases of our lives can short-circuit the decision process. The decision is simple. However, the discernment to ensure that the right choice is made may be compromised. How about in your life – Do you find your decisions, financial or otherwise driven more and more by immediate gratification? What about your relationships – how do you choose the people you spend time with? Do your choices across the day reflect discernment that ensures right decisions are made? What is your reference for, or perspective on choices you face daily as a Christian man? Discuss.

Choice per Webster's New World Dictionary – *to decide or prefer; selection; the right, power, or chance to take an option; think proper.* What does 'choice' bring to mind for you? Do you recall the first time your folks said, 'Son, it's up to you *to decide*'? Did your dad review potential consequences of your *selection*? Did your family ever discuss why God gave us the power of choice to begin with? Share thoughts.

Rate the following for the example set by your dad or father-figure on a scale of 1-10: with 1 being 'bad' and 10 being 'exemplary' on the day to day choices made with his:
- Hobbies and habits;   ___ ___
- Financial management/family budget;   ___ ___
- Establishment of rules and discipline in the home;   ___ ___
- Relationships in the home – in marriage, and with you and
  your siblings; and,   ___ ___
- Walk as a Christian man.   ___ ___

Rate the above again for you today. How do the numbers compare?

The Word on *choice* is:

Scripture – Joshua 24:15, *'But if serving the Lord seems undesirable to you, then choose for yourselves this day whom you will serve, whether the gods your forefathers served beyond the River, or the gods of the Amorites, in whose land you are living. But as for me and my household, we will serve the Lord.'*

- Share a personal story of how a significant choice your dad, or someone close to you made impacted you. Share the influence it has had on the choices you have made in your life.

Reflecting on scripture:

- Have you been to the point where *serving the Lord seems undesirable?*
- Why does Joshua stress to *choose for yourselves this day whom you will serve?*
- Is it possible to serve multiple gods?
- *But as for me and my household, we will serve the Lord.* What was Joshua's choice grounded in?
- Joshua set the standard high as a man, a soldier, a leader, a husband and as a father with choices made across his life. He glorified the Father with his choices and that is his legacy.

Prayer: Lord, do not lead me into temptation, but deliver me from evil. Equip me with discernment and discipline to make the right choice at every point of temptation across the day. Help me recognize temptation for what it is and to lead by example in my walk with You. Amen.

This week I am encouraged to:

_____

_____

_____

_____

_____

_____

_____

_____

26. CONFORM – Not to the world.

As you prepare for this devotion time, prayerfully reflect on a time when you followed a buddy, or a group of friends down a path you wouldn't normally go. Reflect also on the peer pressure experienced during your high school years – did you ever conform in some way to fit in? Do you recall your mom or dad ever saying, 'Don't try to be someone you're not'? Did your parents emphasize knowing who you were and Whose you were? What has influenced your perspective on conformity as a man today? Identify some specifics.

Conform:

Times like these: Soccer and baseball tournaments routinely schedule games for Sunday mornings - church time is compromised. The job requires long hours with travel – family time is compromised. Extending credit lines with relative ease encourages young couples to live beyond their means – self-discipline is compromised. How about in your life – Do you find yourself lowering or re-ordering the core priorities in order to 'fit in'? What about your home – Do the television programs watched reflect priorities you've established? Or does the argument that 'it's just a television show' notch up a victory? What is your reference for, or perspective on conforming to the societal influences you are faced with as a Christian man? Discuss.

Conform per Webster's New World Dictionary – *to be or become the same or similar; to be in accord or agreement; to behave in a conventional way; accepting without question customs, traditions, prevailing opinion.* What does 'conform' bring to mind for you? Do you recall the first time you lobbied to skip that summer buzz hair cut in order to *be the same* as everyone else? Did your dad present the *prevailing opinion* of his day? Was there discussion in your home about the uniqueness of your character and your gifts granted by God? Share thoughts.

Rate the following for your dad or father-figure on a scale of 1-10: with 1 being 'low' and 10 being 'high' on the degree to which he stood firm against pressures to conform with his:
- Circle of friends; ___ ___
- Co-workers; ___ ___
- Balance of time at home and at work; ___ ___
- Priorities on Wednesday night and Sunday; and, ___ ___
- Commitment in marriage and to raising a godly generation. ___ ___

Rate the above again for you today. How do the numbers compare?

The Word on *conform* is:

Scripture – Romans 12:2, *'Do not conform any longer to the pattern of this world, but be transformed by the renewing of your mind. Then you will be able to test and approve what God's will is – His good, pleasing and perfect will.'*

- Share a personal story of a stand your dad, or someone close to you took against the *pattern of this world*. Share the influence it has had on the stands you have taken in your life.

Reflecting on scripture:
- What is the *pattern of this world?*
- How are we *transformed?*
- What is *the renewing of your mind?* Can that be done?
- Can you know *what God's will is* for you?
- Paul is conveying that the tendency to conform to the pattern of this world inhibits the relationship God calls us to. As we are transformed through a relationship with Jesus the Christ, the tendency to conform weakens and the walk with Him strengthens.

Prayer: Lord, too often I let myself be influenced by the world instead of being an influence in the world for You. Transform me by the renewing of my mind through a growing relationship with You, that I may be the influence as the man, husband and father You call me to be. Amen.

This week I am encouraged to:

_____

_____

_____

_____

_____

_____

_____

_____

27. REPENT – Times of refreshing!

As you prepare for this devotion time, prayerfully reflect on a time when you had to come clean on a wrong that you had done. Maybe it was stealing a candy bar; or, possibly more significant like causing damage, physically or emotionally, through some irresponsible action – do you remember accepting responsibility for the wrong done and how you felt at the time? After you confessed, did your parents emphasize setting the wrong right, and committing not to do it again? What has influenced your perspective on repentance as a man today?

Repent:

Times like these: Dad presses on with his long hours at work and misses another school function. He blames the job. A principal works the numbers to improve his school's average test scores. He blames the system. A professional athlete uses banned substances to enhance his performance. He blames the league. How about in your life – Do you find yourself pointing fingers elsewhere when a mistake is made, or do you accept responsibility for it? What about in your home – when frustration percolates to anger, are you able to say, 'I was wrong. I'm sorry. Will you forgive me?' Or does the discussion spiral downward? What is your reference for repentance today? Discuss.

Repent per Webster's New World Dictionary – *to feel sorry or self-reproachful for what one has done or failed to do; to feel such regret or dissatisfaction of some past action, intention, etc. as to change one's mind about; to feel so contrite over one's sins as to change, or decide to change, one's ways.* What does 'repent' bring to mind for you? Do you recall a time when you felt sorry for something you had *done or failed to do?* Did your dad provide encouragement to help you *decide to change one's ways?* Was there discussion in your home about how the Lord calls us to not only confess, but to turn from sin and to God? Share thoughts.

Rate the following for your dad or father-figure on a scale of 1-10: with 1 being 'low' and 10 being 'high' on the degree to which he exemplified repentance for any:
- Offensive actions;   ___ ___
- Habits that may have hurt others;   ___ ___
- Ill-advised relationships, personal or business;   ___ ___
- Disproportionate disciplinary action toward you or other
  siblings; and,   ___ ___
- Wrong choices in his walk as a Christian man, husband or father.   ___ ___

Rate the above again for you today. How do the numbers compare?

The Word on *repent* is:
Scripture – Acts 3:19, *'Repent, then, and turn to God, so that your sins may be wiped out, that times of refreshing may come from the Lord,'*
- Share a personal story of how your dad, or someone close to you repented and turned to God. Share the influence it has had on your walk as a Christian.

Reflecting on scripture:
- Why does Peter instruct us to *repent?*
- The instruction is to *repent, then, and turn...* What are we to turn from?
- Is repentance the only way *sins may be wiped out?*
- Can anything short of a repentant heart claim *times of refreshing...?*
- Sin can be so entrenched in the mind that the only way to break out of it is to come clean, wash thoroughly, turn from it, and fill the void by turning to God.

Prayer: Lord, thank You for Your grace. You know that I sometimes justify a wrong done and press on in my half-truth. But then there You are with the whole Truth to convict me of what is right and just. Grant me the strength and discernment to recognize wrong for what it is; to come clean for any wrong done; and, to turn to You with a repentant heart. Fill me with the times of refreshing that come from You Amen.

This week I am encouraged to:

_____

_____

_____

_____

_____

_____

_____

_____

_____

28. PEACE – Not the absence of war.

As you prepare for this devotion time, prayerfully reflect on a time when you discussed world peace in school or with your family. Did you ever flash the peace sign at your parents during a disagreement; or, possibly when you studied WWII or the Vietnam war in a world history class – do you remember being given a definition of peace? Did your parents provide any clarity to that definition? What has influenced your perspective on peace in the home, community, nation and/or the world today? Identify specifics.

Peace:

Times like these: The events of September 11, 2001, touched the heart of every American – peace in the United States is shaken. Levees breached in New Orleans after Hurricane Katrina flooding the city and essentially making it a war zone – peace in the city is shaken. Dad comes home from work and calls a family meeting to discuss a potential job change – peace on the home front is shaken. How about in your life – Do you find yourself seeking peace, be it peace of mind or peace at work? What about in your home – is there peace? Or does it depend on whether you had a good day or a bad day at the office. What is your reference for, or understanding of peace as a Christian man living in the world? Discuss.

Peace per Webster's New World Dictionary – *freedom from or a stopping of war; freedom from public disturbance or disorder; public security; law and order; freedom from disagreement or quarrels; harmony; concord; an undisturbed state of mind.* What does 'peace' bring to mind for you? Do you recall some *disagreement or quarrels* in your home growing up? Did your dad provide some consequences for disturbing the peace? Are *law and order* necessary for *harmony* to be realized? Was there discussion in your home about how true peace is found only in the Lord? Share thoughts.

Rate the following for your dad or father-figure on a scale of 1-10: with 1 being 'low' and 10 being 'high' on the degree to which he kept the peace:
- in his discussions with family and friends;   ___ ___
- with the rules and discipline in the home;   ___ ___
- during times of conflict;   ___ ___
- while enjoying fun outings; and,   ___ ___
- through his walk as a Christian man, husband and father.   ___ ___

Rate the above again for you today. How do the numbers compare?

The Word on *peace* is:

Scripture – Numbers 6:24-26, *'The Lord bless you and keep you; the Lord make his face shine upon you and be gracious to you; the Lord turn his face toward you and give you peace.'*
- Share a personal story of how your dad, or someone close to you claimed this peace during turbulent times. Share the influence it has had on your walk as a Christian.

Reflecting on scripture:
- Why is it paramount that the *Lord bless you and keep you?*
- How does the *Lord make his face shine upon you?*
- How has the Lord been *gracious to you?*
- What is the significance of having the *Lord turn his face toward you and give you peace?*
- Peace in this passage is a translation of 'shalom', which means, in its most expressive fullness, not the absence of war, but a positive state of rightness and well being in the face of conflict.

Prayer: Lord, You know there is conflict all around – peace seems elusive at times. Grant me the peace You offer in knowing who I am and Whose I am. In Your strength I can maintain a positive state of rightness and well being in the midst of battle and be contagious in my relationship with You. Amen.

This week I am encouraged to:

_____

_____

_____

_____

_____

_____

_____

_____

29. MORALITY – Grounded in the word of God.

As you prepare for this devotion time, prayerfully reflect on a time during your childhood when you were introduced to the concept of right and wrong. Did you lie to your dad or show disrespect to an adult? Do you remember receiving a heart to heart talk on good moral behavior? How did your parents influence your perspective on morality that governs your life today? Identify specifics.

Morality:
Times like these: A Marine General takes a stand that homosexuality is immoral and gets blasted by the media. An editorialist defines morality as 'generally accepted norms and customs' and he gets front page coverage. A dad struggles with his adult son's decision to move in with his girlfriend and hears, 'Everybody does it.' How about in your life – Do you find yourself questioning the status of morality in society, or even in the church? What about in your home – is the moral standard set on Truth? Is there clarity between right and wrong, and an understanding of the associated benefits and consequences? What is your reference for, and stance on morality as a Christian man living in the world? Discuss.

Morality per Webster's New World Dictionary – *moral quality or character; rightness or wrongness, as of an action; the character of being in accord with the principles or standards of right conduct; principles of right and wrong in conduct; ethics.* What does 'morality' bring to mind for you? Do you recall lessons in *rightness or wrongness* in your home growing up? Did your dad help you develop *the character of being in accord with the standards of right conduct?* What were the *standards* based on? Was there discussion in your home about the word of God providing the absolute standard? Share thoughts.

Rate the following for your dad or father-figure on a scale of 1-10: with 1 being 'low' and 10 being 'high' on the degree to which morality was practiced:
  - in his relationships;   ___ ___
  - in his business dealings;   ___ ___
  - in his personal finances, tithing;   ___ ___
  - with Biblical standards set in the home; and,   ___ ___
  - through his walk as a Christian man, husband and father. ___ ___
Rate the above again for you today. How do the numbers compare?

The Word on *morality* is:

Scripture – James 1:21, *'Therefore, get rid of all moral filth and the evil that is so prevalent and humbly accept the word planted in you, which can save you.'*

- Share a personal story of how your dad, or someone close to you stood firm in the Word when the popular trend was going a different direction. Share the influence it has had on your Christian walk.

Reflecting on scripture:

- How do you *get rid of all moral filth?*
- What examples do you face of *the evil that is so prevalent* today?
- How can you *accept the word* of God as absolute when society pushes the word of relativism?
- When, where and how do you nurture *the word planted in you?* What are you to be saved from?
- The word of God, the absolute truth, has been and will continue to be the foundation for morality throughout the ages. Being intentional with time spent in prayer, scripture, worship and study will see the word planted in you take root, sprout, and be an influence for Him in this world.

Prayer: Lord, I know the 'generally accepted norms and customs' of this day reflect the same evil influence present in Biblical times. It can be overwhelming. Help me accept fully the word You have planted in me. Grant me the strength to grow in Your word and equip me with the boldness to be an influence for Your word where You have me, starting with the family You have blessed me with. Amen.

This week I am encouraged to:

_____

_____

_____

_____

_____

_____

_____

30. SACRIFICE – Die a little and live a lot.

As you prepare for this devotion time, prayerfully reflect on a time as a young man when you had to let go of something for the sake of the family. Maybe it was understanding that your family could not afford that new baseball bat you wanted, so you didn't even ask for it. Do you recall being told that sometimes in order to get one thing you might have to give up something else? Did your parents discuss sacrifices made, financial or otherwise, for the sake of the family? What has influenced your perspective on sacrifice at a personal level today?

Sacrifice:

Times like these: A father experiences the ultimate sacrifice, the loss of a son while fighting for our country. A dad turns down a promotion and job transfer for the sake of consistency during the children's school years. Dad and Mom work out a budget to get by on one income, deciding to sacrifice material things instead of family time. How about in your life – are there any sacrifices with the lifestyle you've chosen? What about in your home – are you able to balance time at work and time at home? Or is the tendency to sacrifice time at home for time at work? What is your reference for sacrificial living as a Christian man today? Discuss.

Sacrifice per Webster's New World Dictionary – *the act of offering the life of a person or animal, or some object, in propitiation of or homage to a deity; the act of giving up, destroying, permitting injury to, or forgoing something valued for the sake of something having a more pressing claim.* What does 'sacrifice' bring to mind for you? Do you recall *forgoing something valued for the sake of something having a more pressing claim?* Did your family appreciate your *act of giving up?* What are some examples of sacrificial living in your home growing up? Was there discussion in your home about the sacrifice of Jesus the Christ for our sins? Share thoughts.

Rate the following for your dad or father-figure on a scale of 1-10: with 1 being 'low' and 10 being 'high' on the degree to which he made personal sacrifices:
- with his hobbies; ___ ___
- in his job/career; ___ ___
- with his tithes and offerings; ___ ___
- for his family and home; and, ___ ___
- in his walk as a Christian man, husband and father. ___ ___

Rate the above again for you today. How do the numbers compare?

The Word on *sacrifice* is:
Scripture – Hebrews 10:9-10, *'Then he said, 'Here I am, I have come to do your will.' ... And by that will, we have been made holy through the sacrifice of the body of Jesus Christ once for all.'*
- Share a personal story of how your dad, or someone close to you exemplified selfless sacrificial living. Share how their example has influenced your walk as a Christian.

Reflecting on scripture:
- What is the *will* of the Father for Jesus, His son?
- How have you *been made holy?*
- Why was *the sacrifice of the body of Jesus Christ* necessary?
- What is the significance of *once for all?*
- Read Hebrews 10:1-18 for the whole context of this passage. Jesus walked this earth in selfless service and sacrificial obedience for the sake of our souls. Praise be to God the Father.

Prayer: Lord, I can read these words and I can watch the 'Passion of the Christ', but only by Your grace can I begin to comprehend the sacrificial life You led for me. Through Your obedience to the point of death on the cross, You made the choice clear. And I choose You! Guide me in reflecting Your sacrificial life through my walk as a Christian more tomorrow than today. Amen.

This week I am encouraged to:

_____

_____

_____

_____

_____

_____

_____

_____

_____

31. REJOICE – This day and every day!

As you prepare for this devotion time, prayerfully reflect on a time when you had a particularly joyful experience - maybe it was on vacation with your family, a hike or campsite, or possibly a spiritual experience at baptism or confirmation. Do you recall the feeling? Was it pure excitement, a feeling of freedom or a peace of mind? What is the source of joy in your life today? Identify some specifics.

Rejoice:
Times like these: A dad just can't stop smiling after witnessing the birth of his daughter. Mom and Dad have tears in their eyes as their son walks across the stage on graduation day. A grown man, hardened by life's experiences, breaks down in tears as he accepts Jesus the Christ as his Savior and Lord. How about in your life – are able to rejoice in the gifts and blessings you've received? What about in your home – do you enjoy the blessings of family every day? Or is the tendency to take those blessings for granted and fret about tomorrow? What is your reference for joy-filled living as a Christian man today? Discuss.

Rejoice per Webster's New World Dictionary – *a very glad feeling; happiness; great pleasure; delight; the expression or showing of such feeling.* What does 'rejoice' bring to mind for you? Have you experienced *a very glad feeling, happiness* recently? Did you express your *feelings* or keep your game face on? What are some examples of joy-filled living in your home growing up?

Rate the following for your dad or father-figure on a scale of 1-10: with 1 being 'low' and 10 being 'high' on the degree to which he was able to rejoice in a day:
- with routine activities;   ___ ___
- at work/at the office;   ___ ___
- at home/with family;   ___ ___
- during vacation trips; and,   ___ ___
- on his walk as a Christian man, husband and father.   ___ ___

Rate the above again for you today. How do the numbers compare?

The Word on *rejoice* is:

Scripture – Psalm 118:24, *'This is the day that the Lord has made; let us rejoice and be glad in it.'*
  - Share a personal story of how your dad, or someone close to you exemplified joy-filled living. Share how their example has influenced you.

Reflecting on scripture:
  - What is the significance behind *this is the day?*
  - Who is the Psalmist talking to?
  - How are we to *rejoice and be glad* in these times?
  - Why is it important to recognize this day as *the day that the Lord has made?*
  - This day of rejoicing was made possible by God's deliverance in the victory being celebrated *(NIV Study Bible)*. For the Christian, it is a celebration of the victory over sin through the death and resurrection of Jesus the Christ that we rejoice in at Easter and everyday of our lives.

Prayer: Lord, Thank You for being You. Help me embrace fully the grace offered through Your life, death and resurrection. You have lifted me above the worldly worries and distractions, but I have failed to reflect the joy You have brought into my life through my wife, my family and other relationships. Strengthen my faith and trust in You and deepen my relationship with You by the power of the Holy Spirit, that I may indeed rejoice and be glad in this day and every day by Your grace and for Your glory. Amen.

This week I am encouraged to:

_____

_____

_____

_____

_____

_____

_____

_____

32. THE BODY – Be in shape.

As you prepare for this devotion time, prayerfully reflect on a time when you were introduced to weight lifting - maybe it was motivation from your high school football coach; or maybe you were just trying to impress the girls. Do you recall the feeling as your body responded to a disciplined workout schedule? Did you chart the weight increase at each station across the months? How diligent are you in taking care of your body today? Identify specifics.

The Body:

Times like these: The fast food industry is alive and well providing food with minimal nutritional value. Surgical procedures to address obesity issues are becoming more popular. And some athletes use steroids, human growth hormones and other drugs to enhance their performance. What about in your life – Do you rely on self-discipline for your conditioning routine, or do you look for the quick fix? What about in your home – do you stress nutritional value and home cooked meals? What is your reference for discipline and diligence with the physical body as a Christian man today? Discuss.

Body per Webster's New World Dictionary – *the whole physical structure and substance of a man, animal, or plant; the flesh or material substance, as opposed to the spirit; a group of people or things regarded or functioning as a unit.* What does 'body' bring to mind for you? Do you recall the *physical structure* of the strongest kid in school? Did your coach ever talk about the team *functioning as a unit?* Did your family ever discuss good health, physical strength and conditioning? How about Spiritual health, strength and conditioning? Share thoughts.

Rate the following for your dad or father-figure on a scale of 1-10: with 1 being 'low' and 10 being 'high' on the degree to which discipline and diligence were exemplified daily with:
- his physical health, strength and conditioning; ____ ____
- his spiritual health, strength and conditioning; ____ ____
- his relationship in marriage; ____ ____
- the body of the family as a whole; and, ____ ____
- the body of fellow believers in Christ in the church and community. ____ ____

Rate the above again for you today. How do the numbers compare?

The Word on *body* is:

Scripture – 1 Corinthians 12:12-13, *'The body is a unit, though it is made up of many parts; and though all its parts are many, they form one body. So it is with Christ. For we were all baptized by one Spirit into one body – whether Jews or Greeks, slave or free – and we were all given the one Spirit to drink.'*

- Share a personal story of how your dad, or someone close to you worked with a group from the church to be of service to the community. Share how their example has influenced your walk as a Christian.

Reflecting on scripture:
- What does Paul mean by *the body is one unit?*
- What is Paul referring to when he says, *'though all its parts are many, they form one body'?*
- How do all that believe in Christ become *one body?*
- What is the significance of all being *given one Spirit to drink?*
- Though it is not easy, for its parts are many, we are to form one body in Christ. As the body drinks in one Spirit, the word of God, we can be diligent in the truth and be strengthened as a unit. Outside of truth there is minimal nutritional value, the body is weakened and dysfunctional.

Prayer: Lord, as Your body, we the church seem to be pulling different directions at times. Just as You have instructed me to be disciplined in my physical body, help me to look inside to clearly discern the role You call me to as part of Your body in my family, church and community. As I drink in the Spirit, help me be an influence in this world as a part of Your body. Amen.

This week I am encouraged to:

_____

_____

_____

_____

_____

_____

33. ARMOR – Do not leave home without it!

As you prepare for this devotion time, prayerfully reflect on a time when you were told you needed thicker skin - maybe you took something more personally than you should have or reacted to a situation in an immature way. Do you recall a feeling of vulnerability? How did you 'thicken your skin'? What is your defense today against situations or people that seem to know your areas of vulnerability? Identify specifics.

Armor:

Times like these: Popular television programs sensationalize voting someone off the island, declaring an individual incompetent for a job, and sarcastically criticizing a performer with minimal talent – armor takes some direct hits. A disgruntled employee, mad after a performance review, shoots his boss and then turns the gun on himself – armor was penetrated. What about in your life – Do you know your areas of vulnerability, and where you have defenses built up? What about in your home – do you encourage and equip your family in faith that will deflect the emotional attacks that are part of living in the world? Or is the tendency to go on the offensive with more criticism and even cynicism? What is your reference for a good defense while earning a living in the world as a Christian man today? Discuss.

Armor per Webster's New World Dictionary – *covering worn to protect the body against weapons; any defensive or protective covering; a quality or condition serving as a defense difficult to penetrate.* What does 'armor' bring to mind for you? What *covering* do you wear today to *protect the body against weapons?* How do you build up *a defense difficult to penetrate?* Did your family ever discuss the ultimate *protective covering* in the world? Share thoughts.

Rate the following for your dad or father-figure on a scale of 1-10: with 1 being 'low' and 10 being 'high' on the level of protection he provided in the area of:
- Shelter, food and clothing;   ___ ___
- Financial security for the family;   ___ ___
- His health and well-being;   ___ ___
- Relationship security within marriage and family; and,   ___ ___
- Spiritual grounding in the home and church.   ___ ___

Rate the above again for you today. How do the numbers compare?

The Word on *armor* is:

Scripture – Ephesians 6:10, 14-17 *'Put on the full armor of God so that you can take your stand against the devil's schemes. ... Stand firm then, with the belt of truth buckled around your waist, with the breastplate of righteousness in place, and with your feet fitted with the readiness that comes from the gospel of peace. In addition to all this, take up the shield of faith, ... Take the helmet of salvation and the sword of the Spirit, which is the word of God.'*

- Share a personal story of how your dad, or someone close to you put on the full armor of God in the face of a life challenge. Share how their example has influenced your perspective as a Christian.

Reflecting on scripture:

- Is the *full armor of God* just hardware?
- What is Paul referring to when he says, *'you can take your stand against the devil's schemes'*?
- What are some examples of the *devil's schemes* in your life?
- What is the significance of standing firm in *truth, righteousness, the gospel of peace, faith, salvation and the word of God?* How do some situations or relationships drag you down?
- The full armor of God protects as an impenetrable force against the devil's schemes so that we may be an influence for Him 'in the world' while not becoming 'of the world'.

Prayer: Lord, keep me suited up in Your full armor, that I may indeed stand firm for You as the man, husband and father You call me to be. Work through me, in spite of me to be an influence for you in my family, church and community. Amen.

This week I am encouraged to:

_____

_____

_____

_____

_____

_____

34. RESPONSIBILITY – Following the second Adam.

As you prepare for this devotion time, prayerfully reflect on a time when you were given some responsibility - maybe it was in the form of chores, keeping the yard mowed or getting a job to help provide some income for the family. Did you respond by embracing the responsibility or were you reluctant to accept it? How did Mom and Dad help you understand your responsibilities? How do you respond to the responsibilities associated with life today?

Responsibility:

Times like these: Parents are quick to point fingers at deficiencies in the education system but not as quick to accept responsibility for providing the basic daily discipline and education in the home. Sexual promiscuity is essentially encouraged among young people today while abstinence is scoffed at. Teachings that promote individual responsibility for sexual purity until marriage receive little respect outside the church. What about in your life – Do you embrace responsibilities as they present themselves in the workplace or at church? What about in your home – do you encourage and equip your family with various levels of responsibility in the home? What is your reference for accepting responsibility as a Christian man today? Discuss.

Responsibility per Webster's New World Dictionary *– expected or obliged to account for something, or to someone; able to distinguish between right and wrong and to think and act rationally; readily assuming obligations, duties, etc...* What does 'responsibility' bring to mind for you? When did you show you could ably *distinguish between right and wrong?* Do you always *think and act rationally?* Are you *readily assuming obligations, duties* today? Share thoughts.

Rate the following for your dad or father-figure on a scale of 1-10: with 1 being 'low' and 10 being 'high' on the level to which he embraced responsibilities in the area of:
- Financial provision for the family;   ___ ___
- Discipline - establishing rules for the home, and consequences for breaking those rules;   ___ ___
- Education in school and in the Way;   ___ ___
- Faithfulness in the marriage relationship; being a good role model; and,   ___ ___
- Spiritual leadership in the home, church and community.   ___ ___

Rate the above again for you today. How do the numbers compare?

The Word on *responsibility* is:
Scripture – Genesis 2:15-17 *'The Lord God took the man and put him in the Garden of Eden to work it and take care of it. And the Lord God commanded the man, 'You are free to eat from any tree in the garden; but you must not eat from the tree of the knowledge of good and evil, for when you eat of it you will surely die.'*
- Share a personal story of how your dad, or someone close to you accepted responsibility for who they were and Whose they were. How did their example influence your perspective as a Christian?

Reflecting on scripture:
- Adam was given a *work* to do. What was it?
- With the command came a will to obey. What was Adam responsible for?
- What boundaries are placed on the man's freedom?
- Why will the man *surely die* if he crosses the boundaries given him?
- Adam was given a work to do, a will to obey, and eventually a woman to love in the Garden of Eden. Read Gen.3:6 to see how passively Adam responded to the responsibilities given him.

Prayer: Lord, the first Adam failed to step up to the responsibilities You gave him. Thank You for the second Adam, Jesus the Christ (1Cor.15:45), who did step up to his work of taking on the sins of the world; to his will to obey all the way to the cross; and, to his love for the woman You gave him, the church. I understand what I inherited from the first Adam. Help me step up daily as a man, husband and father in the strength of the second Adam, Jesus the Christ. Amen.

This week I am encouraged to:

_____

_____

_____

_____

_____

_____

_____

_____

35. OBEDIENCE – Yes, Sir!

As you prepare for this devotion time, prayerfully reflect on a time during your childhood when you were given rules to follow. Maybe you were instructed to not ride your bike in the street, or go over to a certain friend's house. As a teenager, you may have been given a curfew. Do you remember obeying the rules, or was there a tendency to push the envelope with disobedience? Did you experience consequences for disobedience? What role does obedience play in your life today? Identify specifics.

Obedience:

Times like these: Folks driving down the road routinely push the envelope and exceed the posted speed limit by 5 to 10 miles per hour. Good law-abiding citizens hire individuals and firms to work every possible angle and aggressively interpret the income tax rules to save some tax dollars. Absolute Truth is under attack by the more socially acceptable relative truth. The consequence is that obedience becomes relative as well. What about in your life – Do you seek to obey the letter of the law or the spirit of the law? What about in your home – Do you draft very specific rules for the home with consequences for disobed-ience? Or are you less specific and more tolerant? What is your reference for obedience at home and in the workplace as a Christian man today? Discuss.

Obedience per Webster's New World Dictionary – *carry out the instructions or orders of; be guided by; submit to the control of.* What does 'obedience' bring to mind for you? Do you remember being told to *carry out the instructions of* someone in charge? Did you have to *submit to the control of* someone? Have you served in a branch of the military? How did that shape your perspective on obedience today? Share thoughts.

Rate the following for your dad or father-figure on a scale of 1-10: with 1 being 'low' and 10 being 'high' on the level of which he embraced obedience in the area of:
- Financial management for the family;   ___ ___
- Self-discipline;   ___ ___
- Effective discipline in the home;   ___ ___
- Faithfulness in the marriage relationship; and,   ___ ___
- Servant leadership in the home, church and community.   ___ ___

Rate the above again for you today. How do the numbers compare?

The Word on *obedience* is:

Scripture – Mark 14:36 *'Abba, Father,' he said, 'everything is possible for you. Take this cup from me. Yet not what I will but what you will.'*
  - Share a personal story of how your dad, or someone close to you stepped up and did something they felt they had to do, even though they didn't want to. How did their example influence you?

Reflecting on scripture:
  - Choosing my will and acting in my strength is of the world;
  - Choosing my will and claiming His strength is idolatry;
  - Accepting His will but acting in my strength is religion;
  - Being obedient in His will and moving forward in His strength is abundant life;
  - Jesus was obedient to the point of death on the cross, clearing the Way to abundant life.

Prayer: Lord, Your word is simple – repent and follow You. Obedience to Your word and Your will is easier said than done. But in Your strength, all is possible. Help me to listen well. Grant me clarity and discernment in Your word, that I may confidently move forward in Your will. Give me the strength needed to stand firm in obedience by the power of the Holy Spirit. Amen.

This week I am encouraged to:

_____

_____

_____

_____

_____

_____

_____

_____

36. ACCOUNTABLE – Got any Battle Buddies?

As you prepare for this devotion time, prayerfully reflect on a time in life when it became clear that you were being held accountable for your actions. Maybe it was having to repair or replace something you damaged; or, maybe it was the first time you were late to work. Do you remember embracing accountability, or was there a tendency to put the blame elsewhere? What role does being accountable to someone, or a group play in your life today? Identify specifics.

Accountable:

Times like these: On the national level we see politicians and pastors fall from grace, and wonder if they were accountable to anyone. At the local level we experience a divorce rate within the church at essentially the same level as outside the church and strive for means to help improve accountability in the marriage relationship. What about in your life – Do you have a friend who holds you accountable? What about in your home – are you willing to say, 'I was wrong. I am sorry. Will you forgive me?' Or is the tendency to blame, even accuse others? What is your reference for being accountable as a Christian man today? Discuss.

Accountable per Webster's New World Dictionary – *to give satisfactory reasons or an explanation; to make satisfactory amends.* What does 'accountable' bring to mind for you? Do you remember being told to *give satisfactory reasons* for a statement made, or action taken? Did you find yourself having to *make satisfactory amends?* Who are you accountable to today?

Rate the following for your dad or father-figure on a scale of 1-10: with 1 being 'low' and 10 being 'high' on the intentional effort made to be accountable to:
- Himself;   _____ __
- The company or individual he worked for;   _____ __
- His friends;   _____ __
- His wife and family; and,   _____ __
- The Body of Christ, the church.   _____ __

Rate the above again for you today. How do the numbers compare?

The Word on *accountability* is:

Scripture – Matthew 18:15-17 *'If your brother sins against you, go and show him his fault, just between the two of you. If he listens to you, you have won your brother over. But if he will not listen, take one or two others along, so that 'every matter may be established by the testimony of two or three witnesses.' If he refuses to listen to them, tell it to the church; and if he refuses to listen even to the church, treat him as you would a pagan or tax collector.'*

- Share a personal story of how your dad or someone close to you exemplified accountability. How did that influence your walk as a Christian?

Reflecting on scripture:

- One-on-one accountability is foundational for understanding and staying in Truth;
- A 'band of brothers' is not easily swayed by the relative truth of the world;
- The Body of Christ, the church, serves as a standard-bearer in His word until Jesus' return;
- What is the difference between 'judgment' and 'accountability'?
- The Lord will take care of judgment in His time. In the interim, brothers in Jesus the Christ are to be accountable to each other in order to navigate faithfully through distractions in the world.

Prayer: Lord, I am an easy target in the world as a lone ranger Christian. I praise You and thank You for the godly men you have brought into my life. Help me be real in those relationships to facilitate a high level of accountability in Truth, that I may be an influence for You in my family, church and community. Amen.

This week I am encouraged to:

_____

_____

_____

_____

_____

_____

_____

37. FORGIVE – Be willing and able.

As you prepare for this devotion time, prayerfully reflect on a time when you were told to forgive someone who had hurt you. Were you physically hurt in a fight or emotionally hurt by some name-calling? Maybe it was a time your dad really lost his temper. Do you remember being willing to forgive, or was it a tough step to take? What role does forgiveness play in your close relationships today? Identify some specifics.

Forgive:
Times like these: A man, unable or unwilling to forgive his wife, files for divorce - A relationship is fractured. A son initiates communication with his dad after years of silence and forgives him for emotional wounds inflicted - A relationship is healed. The Father gives His son so that many will be forgiven - A relationship is desired. What about in your life – Do you have a burden to forgive? Is there a relationship with a dear friend or family member that has been damaged by a reluctance to forgive? What about in your home – Is there encouragement to seek and grant forgiveness? What is your point of reference for forgiveness in the home and at work as a Christian man today? Discuss.

Forgive per Webster's New World Dictionary – *to give up resentment against or the desire to punish; stop being angry with; pardon; to cancel or remit a debt.* What does 'forgive' bring to mind for you? Are you able to *stop being angry* with someone for a statement made, or action taken against you? Or are you inclined to hold onto *resentment, or the desire to punish,* to the point of wanting revenge? Does forgiveness play a role in your relationships today?

Rate the following for your dad or father-figure on a scale of 1-10: with 1 being 'low' and 10 being 'high' – when a wrong was committed, was he able and willing to forgive:
- The company or individual he worked for;   ___ ___
- His friends;   ___ ___
- His extended family;   ___ ___
- His wife; and   ___ ___
- Himself;   ___ ___

Rate the above again for you today. How do the numbers compare?

The Word on *forgive* **is:**

Scripture – Matthew 18:21-22 *'Then Peter came to Jesus and asked, 'Lord, how many times shall I forgive my brother when he sins against me? Up to seven times?' Jesus answered, 'I tell you, not seven times, but seventy-seven times.'*

- Share a personal story of how your dad, or someone close to you exemplified forgiveness and how it impacted the relationships in his life. How did his example impact you?

Reflecting on scripture:

- What is the motivation behind Peter's question?
- Does the seventy-eighth time call for judgment?
- What is Jesus conveying to Peter, and to us?
- Why does forgiveness receive such emphasis at this point of Jesus' ministry?
- Forgiveness is the catalyst for a relationship with Jesus the Christ. Only after we accept the forgiveness He offers and repent can we grow in the relationship He calls us to.

Prayer: Lord, when You taught Your disciples to pray, *'...forgive us our sins as we forgive those who sin against us...'*, You put forgiveness in perspective. Keep me in the Truth that identifies sin as sin and grant me strength to stand firm against the tolerance of sin in my life. Help me embrace the forgiveness You offer, repent and draw closer to You. Teach me to forgive others, that I may love as You love and enable Christ-like relationships in my marriage, my family, the church and community. Amen.

This week I am encouraged to:

_____

_____

_____

_____

_____

_____

_____

38. GUIDANCE – Lead me not into temptation.

As you prepare for this devotion time, prayerfully reflect on a time when you were lost, or separated from your family in a crowd. Maybe you hid too well in a game of hide-n-seek; or weren't paying attention as you were walking and got separated from them. Do you remember that feeling when you first realized you were lost? Do you ever feel lost or like you're going down a road alone today? What guides you through life today?

Guidance:

Times like these: On the national level, our Christian principles are continuously compromised, guiding us down a different road than the one mapped out by our forefathers - A detour is taken. At the local level, an Upward Basketball program guides children and families in the Way - A righteous turn is made. On the personal level, a man stands firm against the relative truth in society and is guided by the absolute truth in the word of God - The next step on the road ahead is clear. What about in your life – What guides you by day? by night? What about in your home – Is there time spent in the word of God? What guidance should be sought in the home and at work today? Discuss.

Guidance per Webster's New World Dictionary *– to point out the way for; direct on a course; conduct; lead; give instruction; train.* What does 'guidance' bring to mind for you? Are you able to *point out the way for* your family? Do you *lead* by example? Do you *give instruction* daily and *train* your children in the Way? What is your reference for guidance today?

Rate the following for your dad or father-figure on a scale of 1-10: with 1 being 'low' and 10 being 'high' for the guidance he provided you in the area of:
- Ethics;   ___ ___
- Priorities;   ___ ___
- Character;   ___ ___
- Truth, the word of God; and,   ___ ___
- Faith and trust in relationship with Jesus the Christ.   ___ ___

Rate the above again for you today. How do the numbers compare?

The Word on *guidance* is:

Scripture – Exodus 13:21-22 *'By day the Lord went ahead of them in a pillar of cloud to guide them on their way and by night in a pillar of fire to give them light so that they could travel by day or night. Neither the pillar of cloud by day nor the pillar of fire by night left its place in front of the people.'*
- Share a personal story of how your dad, or someone close to you provided guidance in your life.

Reflecting on scripture:
- Why did the Lord go *ahead of them* instead of behind them?
- What is significant in the Lord using *a pillar of cloud to guide them?*
- Did the pillar of fire provide about the same visibility they had during the day?
- What does this passage say about God's presence during the Exodus and in our lives?
- God is omnipresent, guiding us every step of the way. All He asks is that we trust Him as He illumines what is in front of us and to let Him guide us through to the journey's end.

Prayer: Lord, when You taught Your disciples to pray, *'...lead us not into temptation, but deliver us from evil...'*, You provided guidance. And then You sent the Holy Spirit as a counselor to keep us on track. Too often I get anxious about tomorrow. Then I am reminded to not worry (Luke 12:22) but to trust in You. Guide me Lord, one step at a time. Strengthen my faith and trust in You on this journey, knowing the destination is eternity with You. Amen.

This week I am encouraged to:

_____

_____

_____

_____

_____

_____

_____

_____

39. CHURCH – One Body and one Spirit.

As you prepare for this devotion time, prayerfully reflect on a time during your childhood when you went to church. What do you remember from your early years in church? Does a particular stained glass window or building as a whole stand out in your mind? Does your pastor or Sunday school teacher come to mind? What was important to you about church early in your life? Identify some specifics.

Church:
Times like these: On the national level, we hear the media tout the separation of church and state almost daily - A lie perpetuates. At the local level, the church is divided between what has been labeled as liberal and conservative teachings - The Truth is compromised. On the personal level, a man sees the church as an institution that he cannot trust - The Body of Christ aches. What about in your life – What do you look for in a church? What attracts you to church? What about in your family – Do you consider the home a dimension of church? What role can the church play in the life of a Christian man today? Discuss.

Church per Webster's New World Dictionary – *a building set apart or consecrated for public worship; public worship; religious service; all Christians considered as a single body.* What does 'church' bring to mind for you? Do you think of *a building set apart?* Do you think of *public worship?* Is your church part of *a single body,* the Body of Christ? What is church to you today?

Rate the following for your dad or father-figure on a scale of 1-10: with 1 being 'low' and 10 being 'high' on his level of engagement in the following church activities or responsibilities:
- Sunday worship;   ___ ___
- Sunday school;   ___ ___
- Physical and financial support;   ___ ___
- Men's ministry; and,   ___ ___
- Lay leader or elder.   ___ ___

Rate the above again for you today. How do the numbers compare?

The Word on *church* is:
Scripture – Ephesians 4:2-6 *'Be completely humble and gentle; be patient, bearing with one another in love. Make every effort to keep the unity of the Spirit through the bond of peace. There is one body and one Spirit – just as you were called to one hope when you were called – one Lord, one faith, one baptism; one God and Father of all, who is over all and through all and in all.'*

- Share a personal story of how your dad, or someone close to you reflected the church at home or work.

Reflecting on scripture:
- Is it natural to be *completely humble and gentle, and patient?*
- What does Paul mean when he says we should be *bearing with one another in love?*
- Does *every effort to keep unity in the Spirit* allow for denominations within the church?
- What is *the bond of peace?*
- God has arranged the parts in the body, every one of them, just as He wanted them to be-1Cor.12:18. Unity in the Body is through relationship with one Lord, in one faith, through one baptism, under one God and Father of all.

Prayer: Lord, I can get caught up in my church versus another church; my denomination versus another denomination. Then I am convicted of how judgmental I can be. Help me find that line between discerning and judging that will keep unity in the Spirit. I know that the peace you offer does not mean the absence of war, but a positive state of rightness and well being in the midst of the battles that are of the world. Strengthen me as a man, husband and father in the church to be completely humble and gentle, to be patient and bear with others in love. Amen.

This week I am encouraged to:

_____

_____

_____

_____

_____

40. GUILT – Let go!

As you prepare for this devotion time, prayerfully reflect on a time during your school years when you were told to go to your room and think about something you had done. What do you remember about that time alone? Did a guilty conscience lead you to a full confession? Or did the guilt just stir up some anger? How did your parents help you deal with guilt growing up? Identify specifics.

Guilt:

Times like these: Accusations fly, fingers are pointed and insinuations of guilt dominate the front page as the media publishes information prematurely - A person or team is guilty until proven innocent. In religious circles, a conviction of guilt can stimulate a man to action - Faith by works is encouraged. On the personal level, the devil knows the guilt buttons to push to make a man feel unworthy - Acceptance of grace is inhibited. What about in your life – What are your guilt buttons? What about in your family – How is guilt dealt with after forgiveness for a wrong has been granted or received? How do you process guilt as a Christian man today? Discuss.

Guilt per Webster's New World Dictionary – *the act or state of having done a wrong or committed an offense; a painful feeling of self-reproach resulting from a belief that one has done something wrong or immoral.* What does 'guilt' bring to mind for you? Have you experienced *a painful feeling of self-reproach?* How do you feel when you have *done something wrong or immoral?* Is there guilt on your heart today?

Rate the following for your dad or father-figure on a scale of 1-10: with 1 being 'low' and 10 being 'high' on the level of guilt he feels, or felt about his life in the following areas:
- Providing effectively for his family;   ___ ___
- Healing damaged relationships with parents and/or siblings;   ___ ___
- Nurturing a happy and healthful marriage and family;   ___ ___
- Achieving a status in life he sought; and,   ___ ___
- Embracing the sacrifice of Jesus the Christ once for all.   ___ ___

Rate the above again for you today. How do the numbers compare?

The Word on *guilt* is:

Scripture – Hebrews 10:22-23 '*let us draw near with a sincere heart in full assurance of faith, having our hearts sprinkled clean from a guilty conscience and our bodies washed with pure water. Let us hold fast the confession of our hope without wavering, for He who promised is faithful;*'

- Share a personal story of how your dad, or someone close to you broke free of a guilty conscience.

Reflecting on scripture:

- What does Paul want us to *draw near* to?
- What is significant about having *a sincere heart in full assurance of faith*?
- Why do you think Paul specifically addressed *having our hearts sprinkled clean from a guilty conscience AND our bodies washed with pure water*?
- If you *hold fast the confession of our hope*, is it possible for guilt to percolate in your mind?
- Guilt is one of the devil's best tools to remind man of his sin. Jesus the Christ provided the sacrifice once for all – 'Their sins and lawless acts I will remember no more.'(Heb.10:17) By His grace guilt is purged with the forgiveness of sin as we *hold fast the confession of our hope*.

Prayer: Lord, forgive my shallow faith that allows guilt to percolate in my mind. What a weak man I am to accept Your blood as adequate to forgive my sins but inadequate to cleanse the guilt from my mind. Grant me the strength to embrace the full assurance of faith and trust in You with a sincere heart, that I may hold fast to the confession of my hope in You by the power of the Holy Spirit. Amen.

This week I am encouraged to:

_____

_____

_____

_____

_____

_____

_____

41. SON – I love you, I am proud of you and I affirm you.

As you prepare for this devotion time, prayerfully reflect on a time when you were reminded that you reflect the family name in all you do. What was the situation? Were you walking into church? Were you competing in a ballgame? Or had you just received a bad grade card? What was to be reflected with the family name? What kind of responsibility was that? What is your responsibility today as an adult in reference to your family name?

Son:

Times like these: It's a boy! The blue bubble gum cigars are passed out and Dad is proud that the family name will be passed on through a son. A boy grows in his unique gifts but faces struggles while seeking approval and encouragement from his dad. A young man wrapping up high school pushes the independence envelope when he is really just seeking validation from his dad as the man he is becoming. What about in your life – Do you remember pushing the envelope with your dad? What were you seeking? What about in your family – Are you encouraging your child to grow in the gifts and strengths he has been blessed with? Are you intentional in affirming your son's development at every stage of his life? Discuss.

Son per Webster's New World Dictionary – *a boy or man as he is related to either or both parents; a male descendant; a son-in-law; a stepson; the Son Jesus Christ, as the second person of the Trinity.* What does 'son' bring to mind for you? Is there a difference between being the *male descendant* of your dad and being *related to* your dad? What does it mean to recognize the Son *as the second person of the Trinity?*

Rate the following for your dad or father-figure on a scale of 1-10: with 1 being 'low' and 10 being 'high' on your dad's experiences as a son. Did he:
- Show you pictures of his parents celebrating his birth;   ___ ___
- Talk of his dad encouraging him in his unique gifts and strengths;   ___ ___
- Share advice his dad had given him about girls;   ___ ___
- Recall becoming a man in his dad's eyes; and,   ___ ___
- Speak of a connection to the Heavenly Father through his father?   ___ ___

Rate the above again for you today. How do the numbers compare?

The Word on *son* is:

Scripture – Mark 9:7 *Then a cloud appeared and enveloped them, and a voice came from the cloud: 'This is my Son, whom I love. Listen to him!'*

- Share a personal story of how your dad, or someone close to you claimed the love of the Father.

Reflecting on scripture:

- The voice that *'came from the cloud'* was that of the _____.
- What is significant about the statement that *'This is my Son,'*?
- Did Jesus need to hear that he was loved by his Father?
- What was conveyed when the Father said, *'Listen to him!'*?
- Every son needs to hear that his father claims him, loves him, affirms him and validates him in who he is becoming.

Prayer: Lord, thank You for being my Heavenly Father, for claiming me, loving me and validating me in who I am becoming. You continue to fill the gap between You and my earthly father, and extend the opportunity to pass a legacy on to my children that will glorify You. Be with me when I fall short as Your representative in my home. Strengthen me in my walk with You and in my walk as a father, that I may become the dad my kids need, the father You call me to be. Amen.

This week I am encouraged to:

_____

_____

_____

_____

_____

_____

_____

_____

_____

_____

42. FREEDOM – In Jesus the Christ.

As you prepare for this devotion time, prayerfully reflect on a time when you were given the freedom to make your own decision. Did it involve taking money out of your savings account? Were you given an upper limit? Or did it have to do with the high school party scene? Did you have a curfew? What kind of freedom was that? What freedoms do you enjoy as an adult today?

Freedom:

Times like these: Freedom of speech is a basic right in these United States that has been practiced all the way to the burning of the flag that represents that freedom. Yet today's 'hate crime' agenda is pushing legislation that could inhibit this freedom all the way to the pulpit. Freedom of religion is another foundational right that protects us from a state religion. Yet the religion of secularism is making significant inroads through the courts, inhibiting this foundational freedom. Freedom of choice is a God-given right first granted to Adam. Yet in the very beginning Adam pushed that freedom beyond its limits and caused quite a ripple effect. What we know is that there are boundaries with freedom, and that consequences result when boundaries are not respected. What about in your life – Do you remember feeling 'free' under your dad's rules? What about in your family – What freedoms do your kids enjoy? What limits have you imposed? Discuss.

Freedom per Webster's New World Dictionary – *exemption or liberation from the control of some other person or some arbitrary power; liberty; independence; release from imprisonment; a being able of itself to choose or determine action freely; a right or privilege.* What does 'freedom' bring to mind for you? Do you remember your first step in *liberation from the control of* your parents? What responsibilities went with being able *to choose action freely?* Was there an event in your life when you realized how freedom was indeed *a right or privilege?*

Rate the following for your dad or father-figure on a scale of 1-10: with 1 being 'low' and 10 being 'high' on how your dad managed freedom in the home. Did he establish boundaries for:
- Making, saving and spending money;   ___ ___
- Language used in the home;   ___ ___
- Hanging out with friends;   ___ ___
- Dating; and,   ___ ___
- Attending church, Sunday school and youth group?   ___ ___

Rate the above again for you today. How do the numbers compare?

The Word on *freedom* is:

Scripture – Galatians 5:1 *'It was for freedom that Christ set us free, therefore keep standing firm and do not be subject again to a yoke of slavery.'*

- Share a personal story of how your dad, or someone close to you embraced the freedom Christ offers.

Reflecting on scripture:

- What *freedom* is Paul speaking of?
- How did *Christ set us free?*
- What are we to be *standing firm* upon?
- What does the *yoke of slavery* refer to?
- Not unlike the Israelites in Egypt, sin has put man in bondage today. But by the blood of Jesus the Christ we can confess, repent, claim freedom in Him, and stand firm upon His word and His love.

Prayer: Lord, thank You for the opportunity to confess and repent of my sin that You will remember no more. Grant me strength in You by the power of the Holy Spirit, to stand firm in Truth against the yoke of slavery that is sin. Lead me not into temptation, but deliver me from evil, for Thine is the Kingdom and the Power and the Glory, forever. Amen.

This week I am encouraged to:

_____

_____

_____

_____

_____

_____

_____

_____

_____

_____

_____

43. RELIGION – Got it?

As you prepare for this devotion time, prayerfully reflect on a time when you felt you 'got religion'. Was it Catholic or Protestant? Were you involved with a specific denomination at the time? Or was it at a non-denominational gathering? Was it a Christian experience? What religion do you practice as an adult today?

Religion:

Times like these: Recently five 'leading thinkers' representing various religions were asked: What is the most dangerous idea in religion today? The Jewish Rabbi answered that it was the insistence that *'My religion is right.'* A Christian representative said it was *'violence in the name of God.'* A naturalist representative said *'a tribal view of God'* is the most dangerous. And another representative suggested it is when a *'follow our rules or else'* mandate is issued. Finally, the Islamic representative said that the initiative of *'converting others to your religion'*, particularly through *'missionary work'* was the most dangerous. These are interesting perspectives. What about in your life – What is your idea of religion? Do you have strong feelings about it? What about in your family – What religion do you subscribe to? Why do you practice that particular religion? Discuss.

Religion per Webster's New World Dictionary – *belief in a divine or superhuman power or powers to be obeyed and worshiped as the creator and ruler of the universe; any specific system of belief, worship, conduct, etc., often involving a code of ethics and a philosophy.* What does 'religion' bring to mind for you? Did your parents have a *belief in a divine power to be obeyed and worshiped?* What *specific system of belief, worship, conduct* was followed in the home? Was there *a code of ethics and a philosophy* associated with the religion your family practiced?

Rate the following for your dad or father-figure on a scale of 1-10: with 1 being 'not at all' and 10 being 'all the time' on how religion was practiced. Did he reflect his religion in his:
- General attitude;   ___ ___
- Dealing with a crisis;   ___ ___
- Commitment to the marriage relationship;   ___ ___
- Relationships inside and outside the family; and,   ___ ___
- Spiritual growth.   ___ ___

Rate the above again for you today. How do the numbers compare?

The Word on *religion* is:

Scripture – John 14:6-7 Jesus answered, *'I am the way and the truth and the life. No one comes to the Father except through me. If you really knew me, you would know my Father as well.'*
- Share a personal story of how your dad, or someone close to you reflected his relationship with Jesus. What impact did that have on your faith?

Reflecting on scripture:
- Why does Jesus say *'the way'* instead of a way?
- What does Jesus mean when He adds, *'..and the truth and the life.'*?
- Isn't it a bit harsh for Jesus to say, *'No one comes to the Father except through me.'*?
- What is significant about the statement, *'If you really knew me, ...'*?
- The Lord calls us not to a religion, but to a growing relationship with Him as we embrace *the truth* that is the word of God, and seek *the life* that is empowered by the Holy Spirit.

Prayer: Lord, You have worked through religion to strengthen my faith in and relationship with You. And at times I have allowed religion to distract me from You. As with the Pharisees in Your day, it is possible to 'get religion' and miss You completely. Help me stay focused on You, that I may really know You better tomorrow than today and be walking a step closer to You each and every day. Amen.

This week I am encouraged to:

_____

_____

_____

_____

_____

_____

_____

_____

44. SERVANT LEADER – By example.

As you prepare for this devotion time, prayerfully reflect on a time when you were asked to do something for your little brother or sister, or to provide a service for your mom and dad. Were you motivated by an allowance, cash money? Or were you satisfied just knowing you had done something to help out? What motivates you to be of service to someone as an adult today?

Servant leader:
Times like these: United States soldiers lead by serving selflessly overseas as men and women have done generations before them to protect the freedoms this country stands for. Firefighters and policemen lead by selflessly laying their lives on the line daily to protect American citizens. Teachers lead by selflessly preparing and reviewing lessons every day across the school year that help educate the minds of tomorrow. What about in your life – Do you know a servant leader? What motivates him or her to lead in service? What about in your family – What examples of servant leadership did you grow up under? What examples are your kids exposed to today?

Servant leader per Webster's New World Dictionary – servant: *a person employed to perform services or duties; a person ardently devoted to another or to a cause, creed, etc.* leader: *a person who leads, directs, commands, or guides a group or activity.* What does 'servant leader' bring to mind for you? Do you think the men signing the Declaration of Independence were *ardently devoted to a cause?* There were certainly servant leaders among our founding fathers, men who were *ardently devoted to a cause* as they stepped up to *lead, direct, command and guide a group* called these United States. Does your home today reflect the spirit of a servant leader?

Rate the following for your dad or father-figure on a scale of 1-10: with 1 being 'not at all' and 10 being 'all the time' on how he practiced servant leadership. Did it show in his:
- Provision for the family;   ____ ____
- Selfless service to the family above and beyond financial provision;   ____ ____
- Love for your mother and partnership with her in parenting;   ____ ____
- Self-less service to the church; and,   ____ ____
- Self-less service to the community?   ____ ____

Rate the above again for you today. How do the numbers compare?

The Word on *servant leader* is:
Scripture – John 13:14-15 *'If I then, the Lord and the Teacher, washed your feet, you also must wash one another's feet. For I gave you an example that you also should do as I did to you.'*
- Share a personal story of how your dad, or someone close to you reflected servant leadership.

Reflecting on scripture:
- What is significant about Jesus validating Himself as *the Lord and the Teacher?*
- Why would Jesus wash His disciples' feet?
- Why did He charge His disciples to *wash one another's feet?*
- What *example* did Jesus provide for the disciples?
- Jesus stooped below even the normal servant's role in washing His disciples' feet, and then charged them as He did in every facet of His ministry to *'do as I did to you'*, be a servant leader.

Prayer: Lord, too often the status quo in leadership roles is to operate in a 'what's in it for me' mode. But you instruct through Paul in Rom.12:2 to *'not conform any longer to the pattern of this world, but be transformed by the renewing of your mind.'* I pray for transformation from a self-centered focus to a selfless focus; from a self-serving leader to a servant leader. Grant me strength to walk a bit closer to You tomorrow than today, to become the servant leader You call me to be, that I may be an influence for You in my family, church and community. Amen.

This week I am encouraged to:

_____

_____

_____

_____

_____

_____

_____

45. CLEAN – Got soap?

As you prepare for this devotion time, prayerfully reflect on a time when you got your mouth washed out with soap. Did you say something that shouldn't have been said? Were you repeating words you had heard but didn't really understand? What 'dirt' was your dad determined to purge from your tongue with soap? How clean is your language today?

Clean:

Times like these: A politician talks about representing the people well and doing what's right upon election, then is distracted by business interests and lobbyists - He loses credibility. A pastor talks of truth and purity, then is distracted by pornography and another woman - He loses his church and his family. The father talks of family as his priority, then gets distracted by work and his favorite hobbies - He loses time he can't get back. Got soap? What about in your life – Are you true to your word in the midst of distractions? Do you walk your talk? What about in your family – In the movie 'Hook' the dad stated that his word was his bond. And his son replied, 'Yeah, junk bonds.' What does your word mean in your home? Discuss.

Clean per Webster's New World Dictionary – *free from dirt, contamination, or impurities; unsoiled; unstained; morally pure; sinless.* What does 'clean' bring to mind for you? What *dirt or contamination* do you deal with everyday? How does a man move through this world of visual stimulation *unsoiled and unstained* spiritually? What provides the grounding for being *morally pure?* Do you think a small accountability group and/or family time together in scripture and in prayer could help you stay clean in word and action?

Rate the following for your dad or father-figure on a scale of 1-10: with 1 being 'not at all' and 10 being 'all the time' on how he worked to stay clean. Did it show in his:
- Schedule, consistently getting home promptly after work;   ___ ___
- Relationships with other men, holding him accountable for who he is and Whose he is;   ___ ___
- Church attendance, striving to grow closer to Christ through worship and study;   ___ ___
- Marriage, honoring and serving his wife; and,   ___ ___
- Words and actions, being a role model at home, church and work.   ___ ___

Rate the above again for you today. How do the numbers compare?

The Word on *clean* is:

Scripture – Num. 8:6-7 *'Take the Levites from among the other Israelites and make them ceremonially clean. To purify them, do this: Sprinkle the water of cleansing on them; then have them shave their whole bodies and wash their clothes, and so purify themselves.'*

- Share a personal story of how your dad, or someone close to you worked to stay clean spiritually.

Reflecting on scripture:

- Why do you think separation *from the other Israelites* was necessary?
- What was important about being *ceremonially clean?*
- What is significant about having *them shave their whole bodies and wash their clothes?*
- Why was it critical for the Levites to *purify themselves?*
- The Levites were charged with work in the tabernacle – it's maintenance and mobility. God made it clear that being clean physically and spiritually was mandatory for Kingdom work.

Prayer: Lord, You know the distractions are many. I can talk the talk, but too often fall short in my walk. The good news is that You are God and that You are not done with me yet. The better news is that You sent Jesus the Christ to wash me clean of sin through His blood on the cross. Help me to fully embrace the grace You have extended to me and strengthen me to stand firm in the full armor of You (Eph.6:10-17) against the distractions in the world, the devil's schemes. I accept responsibility to stay clean and, by Your grace and for Your glory, I will walk closer to You tomorrow than today. Amen.

This week I am encouraged to:

_____

_____

_____

_____

_____

_____

_____

46. TOLERANCE – Respect but do not embrace!

As you prepare for this devotion time, prayerfully reflect on the tolerance your parents had for your attitude and actions during the teenage years. Was their level of tolerance, or lack thereof a good thing? How did it change after you left home? How have your parents impacted the tolerance you practice in relationships with others as an adult? Is there anything you are intolerant of today?

Tolerance:

Times like these: Tolerance is shown to the politician involved in sexual immorality - The line gets fuzzy between personal and professional behavior. Zero tolerance is becoming the norm with alcohol and drug testing in the workplace – The line is clear when liability speaks. Tolerance is granted to homosexuals that profess their 'gay rights' in bold fashion - Any line is perceived as hate-speak. What about in your life – Have you ever felt pressure to compromise your beliefs in the name of tolerance? What are your beliefs based upon? What about in your family – What foundation do you reference during discussions of tolerance in the world today? Discuss.

Tolerance per Webster's New World Dictionary – *to not interfere with; allow; permit; to recognize and respect others' views, beliefs, practices, etc. without sharing them; freedom from bigotry or prejudice.* What does 'tolerance' bring to mind for you? What do you make sure *to not interfere with* in the workplace? Are you able *to recognize and respect others' views without sharing them?* Do you feel others *recognize and respect* your views? Do you think *freedom from bigotry or prejudice* is possible today?

Rate the following for your dad or father-figure on a scale of 1-10: with 1 being 'low' and 10 being 'high' on the level of tolerance conveyed during your formative years for:
- Drugs and alcohol;   ___ ___
- Profane language;   ___ ___
- Sexual immorality;   ___ ___
- Disrespect shown to your mother; and,   ___ ___
- Sleeping in on Sundays.   ___ ___

Rate the above again for you today. How do the numbers compare?

The Word on *tolerance* is:
Scripture – 1Kings 20:42 The prophet said to the king, *'This is what the Lord says: 'You have set free a man I had determined should die. Therefore it is your life for his life, your people for his people.'*
- Share a personal story of how your dad, or someone close to you exemplified tolerance without compromising his faith.

Reflecting on scripture:
- Who had been *set free* and why?
- Why had the Lord determined that the man *should die?*
- Was King Ahab too soft to follow through with the Lord's command?
- Do you think King Ahab understood the Lord's stance in his battle with Ben-Hadad?
- King Ahab showed tolerance for the leader of a polytheistic people the Lord had no tolerance for, and had handed over to him on the battlefield. In His judgment, the consequence was death - *your life for his life, your people for his people.* (read all of 1Kings 20 for full context of the battle)

Prayer: Lord, You are a jealous God with statutes that are to be obeyed. I am convicted that Ben-Hadad represents the proliferation of sin in the world today and that tolerance toward the practice of sin is inconsistent with Your stance on this battlefield. Society often encourages embracing sin, just as King Ahab did, but You have made the consequences for that clear. Guide me in discerning when to be tolerant and when to stand firm in obedience to You. Amen.

This week I am encouraged to:

_____

47. TRUST – In what?

As you prepare for this devotion time, prayerfully reflect on the first time an adult said, 'Trust me.' Were you jumping into the deep end of the pool, or out of a swing? Did they reward your trust? How have your parents impacted the level of trust carried forward in your adult relationships? How easy is it for you to trust others today?

Trust:

Times like these: Baby boomers have good reason to believe that the Social Security system they've paid into all their working lives will collapse before they receive its benefits - Trust in government is compromised. The company's accounting practices drains the pension fund leaving many without the pension they had counted on - Trust in companies takes a hit. The bride and groom draft a pre-nuptial agreement - Trust between a husband and wife is limited to half of the marriage vows, 'from this day forward for better, for richer and in health.' What about in your life – Have you ever been let down by someone you trusted? Have you ever broken the trust someone had in you? What about in your family – Is it obvious in Whom you trust? Discuss.

Trust per Webster's New World Dictionary – *a firm belief or confidence in the honesty, integrity, reliability, justice, etc. of another person or thing; faith; reliance; confident expectation, anticipation, or hope.* What does 'trust' bring to mind for you? What do you have *a firm belief or confidence in?* Do you feel *honesty, integrity and reliability* are characteristics that build trust? Do you place any *reliance* on someone or something? In what do you have *confident expectation, anticipation or hope?*

Rate the following for your dad or father-figure on a scale of 1-10: with 1 being 'low' and 10 being 'high' on the level of trust he built with:
- Co-workers;   ___ ___
- The company he worked for;   ___ ___
- Friends;   ___ ___
- You and your mother; and,   ___ ___
- The church family.   ___ ___

Rate the above again for you today. How do the numbers compare?

The Word on *trust* is:

Scripture – Numbers 14:6-8 *Joshua son of Nun and Caleb son of Jephunneh, who were among those who had explored the land, tore their clothes and said to the entire Israelite assembly, 'The land we passed through and explored is exceedingly good. If the Lord is pleased with us, He will lead us into that land, a land flowing with milk and honey, and will give it to us.'*
  - Share a personal story of how your dad, or someone close to you exemplified trust in a relationship.

Reflecting on scripture:
  - Why were Joshua and Caleb so confident while the ten other spies spread a bad report on the land?
  - What had Joshua and Caleb gained in their time in the wilderness that the others had not?
  - What were the other ten spies placing their trust in?
  - How can two men see opportunity when ten others with them see nothing but obstacles?
  - The Lord had led the people safely out of Egypt, protected them from Pharaoh, provided food and water, and guided them through the wilderness by day and night. Now at the threshold of the promised land, doubt in their own abilities inhibits the trust God had established with them throughout their journey. *(Read Numbers 13 and 14 for full context).*

Prayer: Lord, You are ever-present and worthy of absolute trust. As I look back over my life I see that Your love and guidance have always been present even when I made some wrong turns. Thank You for being there, for being patient with me, for teaching me about trusting in You. I pray that You will *fill me with all the joy and peace as I trust in You*, that I may see beyond self and *overflow with hope by the power of the Holy Spirit (Rom.15:13)*. Amen.

This week I am encouraged to:

_____

_____

_____

_____

_____

48. HOLY – Heavenly focus.

As you prepare for this devotion time, prayerfully reflect on a time during your younger years that you would call a 'holy moment'. Were you receiving your first communion, or being baptized? Or was it a special time alone with God out of doors, taking in all His creation? Did you have any 'holy moments' in your home? How would you rate your personal holiness today?

Holy:

Times like these: After the 9/11 tragedy we saw both houses of Congress, men and women, Republican and Democrat, pray together on the steps of the Capitol – it was a holy moment for our nation's leadership. After the Challenger disaster we saw people across all social, economic and cultural lines stop simultaneously to pray for the families of the seven astronauts – it was a holy moment across our nation. After the tsunami we saw nations around the world step up with aid and in prayer – it was a holy moment across all nations. What about in your life – Are your holy moments frequent? Or are they more likely to follow a personal loss or tragedy? What about in your family – Are you intentional about nurturing personal holiness and increasing the frequency of holy moments in your home? Discuss.

Holy per Webster's New World Dictionary – *dedicated to religious use; belonging to or coming from God; consecrated; sacred; spiritually perfect or pure; untainted by evil or sin; regarded with or deserving deep respect, awe, reverence, or adoration.* What does 'holy' bring to mind for you? What qualifies as *belonging to or coming from God?* What is *untainted by evil or sin?* What gets your *deep respect, awe, reverence or adoration?*

Rate the following for your dad or father-figure on a scale of 1-10: with 1 being 'low' and 10 being 'high' on the practice of the following spiritual disciplines:
- Corporate worship, in church at least every Sunday;   ___ ___
- Bible study and/or Sunday school;   ___ ___
- Reading the Bible;   ___ ___
- Daily time in prayer; and,   ___ ___
- Scripture memorization.   ___ ___

Rate the above again for you today. How do the numbers compare?

The Word on *holy* is:

Scripture – Numbers 16:3-4 *They assembled together against Moses and Aaron, and said to them, 'You have gone far enough, for all the congregation are holy, every one of them, and the Lord is in their midst; so why do you exalt yourselves above the assembly of the Lord?' When Moses heard this, he fell on his face;*

- Share a personal story of how your dad, or someone close to you exemplified personal holiness.

Reflecting on scripture:
- What was the assembly suggesting when Korah said *all the congregation are holy?*
- Did the congregation have grounds to claim *the Lord is in their midst?*
- What do you think about Moses' response to this confrontation?
- What was the assembly's motivation in taking a stand against Moses and Aaron?
- The assembly was selfishly grasping holiness outside the will of God. Moses was selflessly seeking holiness in the will of God. *(read the balance of chapter 16 to see God's response)*

Prayer: Lord, my holy moments too often occur after tragedy or personal loss. Such a low frequency, even complimented by church attendance, gives the devil no cause for concern. I allow him to continue bombarding me with a higher frequency of world moments. Grant me diligence in practicing Your spiritual disciplines to gain the spiritual strength and stand firm against the devil's schemes. Guide me in my walk toward greater personal holiness, that I may see every moment as a holy time with You, by Your grace and for Your glory. Amen.

This week I am encouraged to:

---

49. CONSEQUENCE – Truth, or else!

As you prepare for this devotion time, prayerfully reflect on a time during your childhood when you were told, 'There will be consequences for your actions.' Had you told a lie, or failed to do your chores? Had you stolen a candy bar from the store and got caught? What consequences were incurred as a result of your actions? Are there consequences for your actions today?

Consequence:

Times like these: A dad rolls through a stop sign in his neighborhood – no apparent consequence, but his son is watching. A dad in a hurry and driving a bit fast runs a red light and mumbles about the city's bad timing sequence for their stop lights – no apparent consequence, but his son is watching. A young man runs a red light and is hit broadside by another vehicle in the intersection – the consequence is apparent as a dad mourns. What about in your life – Are consequences always apparent? Have you ever gotten away with something only to find out later that there were still consequences? What about in your family – Are there rules established for the home? Are consequences for breaking those rules clear, agreed upon and enforced? Discuss.

Consequence per Webster's New World Dictionary – *a result of an action, process; outcome; effect; a logical result or conclusion; inference; the relation of effect to cause.* What does 'consequence' bring to mind for you? When a law is written, is there a desired *result of an action?* When rules are established, is it *a logical result* to expect obedience? Is the *relation of effect to cause* always clear? Are consequences compromised in our legalistic society?

Rate the following for your dad or father-figure on a scale of 1-10: with 1 being 'low' and 10 being 'high' on the communication and enforcement of consequences when you:
  - Did something you were instructed not to do; ___ ___
  - Showed disrespect to your mom; ___ ___
  - Bypassed your chores or other responsibilities to do what you wanted to do; ___ ___
  - Failed to give your best effort academically or athletically; and, ___ ___
  - Rolled through a stop sign physically, emotionally or spiritually. ___ ___

Rate the above again for you today. How do the numbers compare?

The Word on *consequence* is:
Scripture – 2Samuel 12:10 *'Now, therefore, the sword will never depart from your house, because you despised Me and took the wife of Uriah the Hittite to be your own.'*
- Share a personal story of how your dad, or someone close to you incurred consequence for an action.

Reflecting on scripture:
- Why did the Lord send Nathan to rebuke the actions of King David?
- What is meant by *the sword will never depart from your house?* Is this a consequence?
- How has Kind David *despised* the Lord?
- Was this all tied to David's sin with Bathsheba?
- There was no apparent consequence when David took his second wife, his third wife, or even his eighth wife. But when lustful behavior continues unchecked, the consequences are dire.

Prayer: Lord, consequences help me stay on the narrow path while the lack thereof allow me, even encourage me to go down quite a different path. In our legalistic times consequences for breaking rules are minimized whether they be rules of law, or Your commandments. Help me be obedient and embrace consequences in my life as behavior modification that will open the door to deeper relationship with You. Guide me and be with me that I may become the man, husband and father You call me to be, by Your grace and for Your glory. Amen.

This week I am encouraged to:

_____

_____

_____

_____

_____

_____

_____

50. JEALOUSY – Righteous or unrighteous?

As you prepare for this devotion time, prayerfully reflect on a time when you were jealous of a friend's stuff. Was it a bicycle or a ball glove? Was it his house? Maybe it was even his family, the way his dad was always involved and supportive. How did your jealousy effect your friendship? What stirs feelings of jealousy in you today?

Jealousy:

Times like these: A dad works 80 hour weeks striving to climb the career ladder, jealous of the success of his colleagues. A jealous husband reacts negatively when a co-worker talks to his wife at a company gathering. A man struggles with the calm his Christian friend exhibits in the midst of personal tragedy, jealous of the faith and trust he doesn't have. What about in your life – Is jealousy a motivator for you? Is it just about material possessions and social status? What about in your family – Are feelings of jealousy common topics of discussion? Should they be? Discuss.

Jealous per Webster's New World Dictionary – *very watchful or careful in guarding or keeping; resentfully suspicious of a rival or a rival's influence; resentfully envious; requiring exclusive loyalty.* What does 'jealousy' bring to mind for you? Would others say you are *very watchful or careful in guarding* your relationships? Have you ever been *resentfully suspicious of a rival?* Have you been *resentfully envious?* What in your life requires *exclusive loyalty?*

Rate the following for your dad or father-figure on a scale of 1-10: with 1 being 'low' and 10 being 'high' on his feelings of jealousy toward:
- The 'Joneses' next door;   ___ ___
- Superiors in the office, or supervisors at work;   ___ ___
- Apparent financial well being of others;   ___ ___
- A relative, or another family that seems to 'have it all together'; and,   ___ ___
- A friend's faith and trust in the Lord.   ___ ___

Rate the above again for you today. How do the numbers compare?

The Word on *jealousy* is:

Scripture – Numbers 25:11-13 *'Phinehas the son of Eleazar, the son of Aaron, the priest, has turned away My wrath from the sons of Israel in that he was jealous with My jealousy among them, so that I did not destroy the sons of Israel in My jealousy. Therefore, say 'Behold, I give him My covenant of peace; ... because he was jealous for his God and made atonement for the sons of Israel."*

- Share a personal story of when your dad, or someone close to you was stimulated by jealousy to grow in their faith. What impact did that have on you?

Reflecting on scripture:

- What is meant by *jealous with My jealousy?*
- How is God justifying action in His *jealousy?*
- Is *My covenant of peace* established in the absence of jealousy or the presence of jealousy?
- Is Phinehas righteous *because he was jealous for his God?*
- I the Lord your God am a jealous God, punishing the children for the sin of the fathers to the third and fourth generation of those who hate me.(Ex.20:5) Phinehas understood the Lord's jealousy.

Prayer: Lord, I have been jealous of many people and things in my life. I am convicted by Your word: My unrighteous jealousy is not of You, but indeed contrary to You. Your statutes dictate that I 'shall not worship any other god, for the Lord, whose name is Jealous, is a jealous God.' (Ex.34:14) In Your righteous jealousy, help me stand firm under Your influence and against the influence of other gods in my life, by Your grace and for Your glory. Amen.

This week I am encouraged to:

----

51. PASSIVITY – To be rejected!

As you prepare for this devotion time, prayerfully reflect on a time when you were passive while others did something wrong. Were your buddies picking on other kids? Did you let your best friend see your answers on a test? Or did you stand by while a friend twisted instructions from his dad to justify doing what he wanted to do? Were there consequences or any lessons learned? In what ways are you passive today?

Passivity:

Times like these: Several court cases across the country have called for removing displays of the Ten Commandments from public places – too often, we the people are passive in the face of spiritual responsibilities our forefathers embraced. Reports indicate individual debt is increasing while savings decrease – too often, we are passive about financial responsibilities. Statistics show that four of ten kids wake up in homes without a dad present – too often, men are passive about their fathering responsibilities. What about in your life – Is passivity an issue in any area of life? What do you stand for? What about in your family – Have you been a passive father or have you fully embraced your responsibilities? Discuss.

Passivity per Webster's New World Dictionary – *influenced or acted upon without exerting influence or acting in return; offering no opposition or resistance; submissive; yielding; patient; taking no active part.* What does 'passivity' bring to mind for you? Have you caught yourself being *influenced without exerting influence in return?* When various media enter your home, do you find yourself *offering no opposition or resistance?* Are you active in, or do you take *no active part* in the local, state, or federal political process?

Rate the following for your dad or father-figure on a scale of 1-10: with 1 being 'passive' and 10 being 'active' toward:
- Mom's 'to do' list;   ___ ___
- His responsibilities at work;   ___ ___
- Your interests and activities;   ___ ___
- Community needs and the political process; and   ___ ___
- Conducting a family devotional and leading the way to church.   ___ ___

Rate the above again for you today. How do the numbers compare?

The Word on *passivity* is:

Scripture – Genesis 3:6 *'When the woman saw that the fruit of the tree was good for food and pleasing to the eye, and also desirable for gaining wisdom, she took some and ate it. She also gave some to her husband, who was with her, and he ate it.'*
- Share a personal story of when your dad, or someone close to you took a stand when a wrong was done. What impact did that have on you?

Reflecting on scripture:
- Was the eating of the fruit what caused the fall of man, or did the man stumble before that?
- Who received instructions to not eat from the tree of the knowledge of good and evil? (Gen.2:17)
- Where was Adam when the serpent was deceiving his wife?
- Why didn't Adam stand in the gap between his wife and the serpent?
- Passivity by Adam toward instructions given him by God is arguably man's first sin. In his failure to accept responsibilities granted him, he allowed Eve to eat the forbidden fruit.

Prayer: Lord, I have been passive in many areas of my life. None more so than in my walk with You. Grant me the strength to reject passivity and to pursue a deeper relationship with You. I want to be passionate in my walk with You, reflecting Your love and standing firm for Your righteousness in my home, in my church and in my community. Guide me on that path. Amen.

This week I am encouraged to:

_____

_____

_____

_____

_____

_____

_____

_____

52. COURAGEOUS – Doing what is right.

As you prepare for this devotion time, prayerfully reflect on a time when you were told, 'That took courage!' Were you standing up for a friend that couldn't stand up for himself? Did you take a stand against pressure from your peers? How did your parents influence your ability to courageously take a stand? In what ways are you courageous today?

Courageous:

Times like these: A politician waits for poll results before taking a stand on the issue – not very courageous decision-making in government. A soldier presses on following orders for the front line to take the next ridge – courageous obedience in battle. A pastor preaches scriptural truth boldly from the pulpit in the face of popular trends – courageous leadership in the Body of Christ. What about in your life – Are you firm in your faith and convictions? Or do you go with the flow? What about in your family – How do you lead courageously as a dad? Discuss.

Courage per Webster's New World Dictionary – *the attitude of facing and dealing with anything recognized as dangerous, difficult, or painful, instead of withdrawing from it; quality of being fearless or brave; valor; mind; purpose; spirit; to do what one thinks is right.* What does 'courage' bring to mind for you? Do you think of Stormin' Norman and our soldiers on the front lines of battle during the first Gulf War? Do you think of firefighters working to save victims trapped inside a burning building? What are you facing today that is *recognized as dangerous, difficult or painful?* Are you *withdrawing from it,* or standing up for what you *think is right?*

Rate the following for your dad or father-figure on a scale of 1-10: with 1 being 'low' and 10 being 'high' on his practice of leading courageously. Did he:
- Serve in the United States military;   ___ ___
- Step up as a Scout leader in your den and troop;   ___ ___
- Exemplify and expect good sportsmanship on the field;   ___ ___
- Conduct a family devotional in the home; and   ___ ___
- Facilitate a Bible study or Sunday school at church?   ___ ___

Rate the above again for you today. How do the numbers compare?

The Word on *courageous* is:
Scripture – Joshua 1:7 *'Be strong and very courageous. Be careful to obey all the law my servant Moses gave you; do not turn from it to the right or to the left, that you may be successful wherever you go.'*
   - Share a personal story of when your dad, or someone close to you showed great courage facing a trial. What impact did that have on you?

Reflecting on scripture:
   - Why did Joshua have to be *strong and very courageous?*
   - Was God referring to physical, emotional or spiritual strength?
   - What is the significance of following *'Be strong and very courageous.'* with *'Be careful to obey '*?
   - What foreign gods posed a threat to Israel, to turn them *to the right or to the left* of the Law?
   - Joshua needed all his physical, emotional and spiritual strength to muster the courage to obey the Law himself and lead in the Law as the Israelites took possession of the land beyond the Jordan.

Prayer: Lord, just as in Joshua's day, many gods are at work trying to turn my eyes from You. Grant me the physical, emotional and spiritual strength to courageously stand in Your truth. Help me be the man, husband and father that will lead the way for my family, church and community. Equip me to be an influence in this world with courage grounded in You. Amen.

This week I am encouraged to:

_____

_____

_____

_____

_____

_____

_____

_____

About the Author

Rick Wertz is the founder and president of the Faithful Fathering Initiative in Texas. He is a graduate of the University of Kansas with a degree in Mechanical Engineering. He also completed graduate level training on the Dimensions of Fathering from Abilene Christian University as well as further training conducted by the National Center for Fathering in Shawnee Mission, Kansas. He lives with Linda, his bride of nearly 30 years, in Sugar Land, Texas. They have two college-age children.

Rick spent 15 years in the corporate world, moving his family eight times while he focused on the career ladder and financial security. When he received a wake-up call as to how out of balance his life had become, the focus was turned to his walk as a father and with the Father. Many blessings, even answers to prayers from his youth, were being taken for granted as he strove to be successful. The ninth move was out of the corporate world and to Sugar Land, Texas, where he and Linda committed themselves to stay and raise the children through their high school years.

Rick's personal wake up call matured into a calling to do more. In May, 2000, he founded FFIT. Inspired by his experience, and with the help of the Board of Directors, the not-for-profit organization was established with the mission *to encourage and equip dads in their role as a father, to become heroes of the next generation.*

Rick's ability to blend his practical experience with the application of the word of God on his journey as a man, husband and father has made him a popular speaker, teacher and facilitator. His passion is contagious as he partners with churches, businesses and other organizations to conduct workshops for dads, small group studies and father/daughter & father/son retreats. Whether with a small group, large group or on the radio as a talk show guest, Rick's focus is always on encouraging and equipping men from all walks of life to have a positive impact one family, one church, one community at a time.

To contact Rick Wertz or request information about the Faithful Fathering Initiative in Texas:

        Call: 281.491.DADS (3237)
        Email: Rick@faithfulfathering.org
        Visit: www.faithfulfathering.org
        Write: FFIT, P.O. Box 1702, Sugar Land, TX 77487